# Basic Understanding of the Stock Market

## For Teens and Young Adults
## Book Four

**By Ronald E. Hudkin**

D1413644

## Description

Basic Understanding of the Stock Market for Teens and Young Adults is for anyone new to investing in the stock market who is looking for a simplified scaled down reference point to make sure you understand your investments and strategies. This book provides you with the information you need to protect and grow your stock investments in today's changing market.

Whether you are a completely new investor or simply confused about all the contradictory advice out there, this book is an accessible guide to understanding how to grow your money a smart and easy way.

You will learn Stock Market Basics as this book is aimed at the individual investor who wants to understand today's stock market and make wise investment choices based on knowledge and understanding of the overall picture. It is written in easily understandable terms and gives a clear explanation of how all the pieces fit together in the marketplace. Readers will better understand the detailed, practical and working knowledge of the stock market necessary to become a success.

It is a perfect match for those with no experience or background, as well as for the experienced investors that lack the optimal skills for active stock trading. It will give you an understanding how to become financially independent and put you in control of your own destiny. Basic Understanding of the Stock Market for Teens and Young Adults belongs on the bookshelf of anyone who is new to investing or simply wants a broader understanding of the market.

In this book, you will not find any secret formula or long lost potion to earn millions in the stock market, but after reading this book your comprehension of the stock market will go to an actual understanding. This book will help you understand exactly what that guy in the top notch suit is saying about where to put your money and help you make your own decision, after all it's your financial destiny. This book will not make you a market expert tomorrow, but it will honestly help you to understand the stock market a whole lot better. This book will show many investing options and help you to put together a realistic portfolio that takes control of our own investments!

Basic Understanding of the Stock Market for Teens and Young Adults is ready to share a wealth of information with you. Get it now.

**Financial Disclaimer**

## DEDICATION

I dedicate this book to teens and young adults looking for sound advice on how to make smart financial choices needed to establish a firm footing as you work your way through school and the post-graduation years.

Just remember as your speeding down that new found road of freedom that how you spend your 20's financially will ultimately define you.

After all is said and done you should also know; after you get married, someone should know how to write a check correctly, save and invest. Because, even if you have tons of love, there's still going to be a lot of bills!

# Table of Contents

**Title Page**

**Copyright**

**Description**

**Financial Disclaimer**

**Dedication**

**Chapter One - General Overview**

What is a Stock?

Is the Stock Market Legalized Gambling?

Why Invest in The Stock Market?

Why People are Afraid to Invest in Stocks?

Why Would I Choose Stocks?

How Old Do You Have to Be to Buy Stocks?

What are the Main Types of Stocks?

Where Do I Buy Stocks?

When is the Best Time to Invest?

**Chapter Two - Types of Stocks**

What Are Penny Stocks?

What Are Common Stocks?

What Are Preferred Stocks?

What Are Dividend Stocks?

What is a Cyclical Stock?

What is a Blue Chip Stock?

**Chapter Three – Market Orders**

What Are Some of the Orders I Can Place?

What is a Market Order?

What is a Stop Loss Order?

What is a Cover Order?

What is an After Market Order?

What Are Normal Orders?

**Chapter Four – Board, Stock Indexes, Sectors and Markets**

What is the Big Board?

What is the Dow Jones or the DJIA?

What is the NASDAQ?

What is the S&P 500?

What are Agriculture Stocks?

What are Insurance Stocks?

What are Energy Stocks?

What are Bank Stocks?

What is a Bull Market?

What is a Bear Market?

What is a Market Crash?

**Chapter Five – Investing Online**

How Can I Open an Online Account?

How to Fund My Online Account?

Do I Need to be a Computer Expert?

How Can I Overcome my Fear?

What Determines a Stock's Price?

**Chapter Six General Investment Questions**

What is the Difference between Growth and Value Investors?

What is Speculative Investment?

How Do I Know I Make the Right Investment?

Why Should I Invest in Different Stocks?

What are the Best Long-term Investment Strategies?

What Do Stock Investors Really Need?

What are the Best Reasons I Need to Invest?

Why Should I Invest Regularly?

What are the Rules of Investing?

What are the Guides of Choosing a Good Investment?

What are Common Investment Vehicles?

What Should I Do to Develop the Right Mindset?

Difference between Bull and Bear Markets

What is Insider Trading?

What are Advances and Declines?

What are Bid and Ask Prices?

What is Short Selling?

What is a Dividend?

What is the P.E. Ratio?

What are Stock Split and Reverse Stock Splits?

What is Dollar Cost Averaging?

What is a Margin Account?

**Chapter Seven – Swing Trading**

What is Swing Trading?

How to Get Started in Swing Trading

What is the Difference between Swing and Day Trading?

What's considered a Good Swing Trading Return?

**Chapter Eight – Day Trading**

What is Day Trading?

How Much Money is needed to Start Trading?

How to Start Day Trading

**Chapter Nine – Stock Instruments Traded**

What are the Instruments Traded in the Stock Market?

Stocks VS Mutual Funds

Difference between Growth and Value Investors

Common Stocks vs Preferred Stocks

What is a Stock Option?

What is a Mutual Fund?

What is a Mutual Fund's N.A.V.?

What is a 401k Plan?

What is an IPO?

**Chapter Ten – Reports and Analysis**

What is a Stock Market Technical Analysis?

What is a Technical Analysis?

What is a Fundamental Analysis?

How is a Fundamental Analysis Done?

What is an Annual Report?

What is listed in an Annual Report?

How Do I Obtain an Annual Report?

**Chapter Eleven – Stock Investing Tips**

What to do When the Market is down

How to Avoid Common Mistakes as a Beginner

How to Grow Money in the Stock Market

How Do You Know You Are Starting Right

When is the Market Open?

How Much Return Can I Expect?

How Do I Know Which Stocks to Buy?

How Can I Track Stocks?

How to Make Money in Stocks

Tips to Grow Your Money in the Stock Market

What is the Best Single Savings Tip?

What are the Basic Steps in Managing My Money?

How Can I Stop My Bad Savings Habit?

What Are Somme Tips on Money Management?

**Chapter Twelve – Miscellaneous**

Is Stock market Investing Good for Retirement?

How Much Money is needed to Buy Shares of a Company?

Aside from Reading What Else Do I Need?

Can I Retire a Millionaire?

Why Do I Need to Have Big Dreams?

Will Somebody Always Buy My Stocks When I Sell?

What Are the Best Ways to Make Money With Stocks?

**Appendix I - Worthless Stock: How to Avoid Doubling Your Losses**

**Book Review**

**About the Author**

**Other Books**

**Investing for Profit**

**References**

## Chapter One
## General Overview

### What is a Stock?

The term 'stock' is commonly used in investment spheres but not many people may be able to define what it is. A stock represents a share of ownership in a listed company. A stock is a claim on a firm's earnings and assets. When you purchase more stocks, your ownership stake in the company becomes higher. When you buy a company's stock, it implies you are recognized as one of the company owners and because of this, you have a small portion of claim to every asset an establishment owns. When you purchase a stock, you own every piece of trademark, furniture and contract of an organization. Since you are an owner, you have the freedom to share a firm's earnings as well as participate in voting exercises that are directly related to the stock.

When you purchase a stock, you are given a stock certificate that serves as proof of your ownership. In the past, a stock certificate was a fancy piece of paper. However, with modern technology, these documents are stored electronically also called holding shares. Electronic storage makes the work of a stock broker much easier. In the past, if you wanted to sell your shares, you were supposed to physically hand-in your certificate to the brokerage firm to facilitate transaction. In this new day and age, click and mouse trading has made life easier for everyone.

When you purchase a stock in a public firm, this doesn't mean you have full rights to day to day operations of a business. However, you get a chance to exercise your freedom in a firm during times when elections for a board of directors are held. It's worth mentioning that buying a stock doesn't mean you have the exclusive right to decide how an organization should run its operations.

It is the responsibility of the management of a company to ensure that shareholders' investments are protected and the value of a company stock goes up. When this fails to happen, shareholders reserve the right to vote the management out and elect new ones. However, the truth of the matter is that some companies break these rule and minor shareholders often don't have enough power to influence a company's operations. In most cases, individual billionaires and institutional investors are the ones whose voice is heard because they have invested heavily in a company.

For an ordinary shareholder, your interest will not be really to manage a company but rather hope that the firm is managed well so that you can make money from your investment. As a shareholder, you are set to receive profits obtained by a firm and have a claim on assets. Company profits are paid out to shareholders in form of dividends. The higher the amount of shares you own, the more profit you receive when dividend payouts are done. You can only claim a share of assets when the company you have invested in goes bankrupt. In the event of liquidation, you receive payments after payments to all creditors have been settled.

It's worth mentioning that limited liability is an important feature for any stock. This implies that as a stock owner, you are not accountable and responsible in the event of a company failing to honor its debts. Other companies such as partnerships are established in such a way that in case the partnership declares bankruptcy, creditors are allowed to pursue partners in their individual capacity in order to recover their property. When you purchase a stock, it means that the only thing you are at risk of losing is the value of your investment. In the event that a company you were a shareholder goes down, nobody can come to you and claim your personal assets.

Before purchasing stocks, it is important to understand what they are as well as your duties and obligations as a stock holder. Knowing what a stock is also helps you to understand your rights as a shareholder. Of course, just like any other venture, it is important to first research thoroughly on your available investment options before making a decision. In case you are planning to buy stocks, there are several options out there. You can either research by yourself or seek the services of a qualified investment analyst.

**Is the Stock Market Legalized Gambling?**

A lot of people think twice about getting into the stock market because they believe it is similar to gambling. We are living in hard economic times where everyone is looking for a way to make extra money and secure their financial future. Because of the high standards of living and financial pressure, some people opt for methods such as gambling in order to earn money. While some people believe investing in the stock market cannot be equated to gambling, others believe otherwise. To understand the difference between gambling and whether the stock market is a legalized form of gambling, it is vital to know what each definition involves.

It's important to mention that both investing and gambling involve putting money into use with a hope of getting back more. The dictionary meaning of gamble is highly associated with games which has no association whatsoever with stock investing. Therefore, it is accurate to conclude that gambling is closely associated with games and entertainment but with the aim of making a better return on the initial investment. On the other hand, investing in the stock market is all about business. It's good to mention that in some countries, gambling is outlawed and therefore, those found engaging in this practice are reprimanded by the law. On the other hand, stock investing is a business investment practice that is legal across the globe. Based on this explanation, stock investing is purely a business activity and cannot therefore be referred to as legalized gambling.

For gamblers, their ultimate aim is to reap as much money as possible after playing a game. However, for stock investors, they don't aim for immediate profits but rather, wait until the markets become favorable to allow them make good returns. In other words, it could take months or years before you finally make good financial returns.

The purpose of engaging in gambling and the stock market is totally different. A lot of gamblers engage in this activity in order to make money for leisure activities. However, the stock market is used by investors to grow their investment in order to spend it productively. Investing in stocks is a serious affair and can therefore not be associated with any gambling techniques. Stock market investment is a long term affair while gamblers do it for short term excitement by putting their money at risk and hope for a chance that it will turn around their financial fortunes. However, despite the differences, there are a few things that both gambling and stock investing share in common. To begin with, they both involve the use of money in form of an investment whose return is not known. In other words, they are associated with both the risk of time and money. The stock market shouldn't be at any one time confused with gambling whether legal or not because the two operate differently. It is important for the difference between the two to be clearly defined to avoid sending out the wrong perceptions.

## Why Invest in The Stock Market?

With the current economic state and the high costs of living, a lot of people prefer to safeguard their future by finding a way to save and improve their financial status. In the recent times, the stock market has become a popular investment choice for many individuals. First and foremost, the stock market is versatile and offers you plenty of choices to choose from. Shares, debentures, bonds and securities are some of the common stock market options available. This is an advantage because it means you have plenty of investment opportunities for your money. The stock market is a place where you can grow your investment over time and reap handsome benefits in the coming days.

## Why People are Afraid to Invest in Stocks?

Stocks are one of the most common investment plans that many people think about. The current economic meltdown and rising costs of living have forced investors to go a notch higher and consider diversifying their investments in order to secure their financial future. There are different types of stocks and it is important for every investor to make an effort and understand what the industry is all about. Because of the volatile nature of stocks, a number of people are always afraid to put their money in stocks. Stocks prices fluctuate rapidly and are always affected by prevailing circumstances and other happenings in the market.

Because of the risks associated with stocks, only investors who can tolerate high levels of risk have been able to succeed in this industry. The fear of losing money is what drives away investors from the stock market. However, it is good to note that despite the challenges of the stock market, there is a high chance of making good returns especially if the right investment decisions are made. It's worth mentioning that the stock market is just like any other investments that come with their own risks.

The process of choosing the right company and stock to invest in scares away many people. The fear of committing mistakes as a beginner is one of the contributing factors why some investors prefer not to take the bold step to become stock investors. In order to overcome this fear, it is important for investors first and foremost, understand their level of risk tolerance. The problem is that a lot of people get into stock investment without first understanding how much risk they are willing to tolerate. This is a mistake because every negative trend or happening in the stock industry is a source of stress and frustration.

A lot of theories have been put forward about stock investing. While some people find it to be a risky business that is not worth investing, others have had their financial fortunes turn around for the better thanks to stock investing. The best way to overcome fear associated with stock investing is to make sure that you are well informed and have received the appropriate advice before investing. Some people get misadvised and think that the stock market is a quick way to get rich only to be disappointed when stock prices decline.

Having the right information and understanding well in advance the risks associated with stock investing prepares you for the experience. The best way to deal with fear associated with stocks is to begin your investment with a small amount of money. Ideally, the amount of money you decide to invest should be extra income that is not meant of bills or any other crucial expenses such as medical and school fees. By investing in a small amount you are comfortable with, you are sure that in case anything goes wrong, you're still in a good financial position to cater for your other expenses.

## Why the Stock Market is the Best Choice for You

- Perfect Opportunity to Increase your money: Everyone who comes to the stock market has one goal in mind – to increase their money and build a solid financial base. When you invest in stocks, you get the perfect chance to increase your investment especially when stock prices rise in value. So long as you have invested in a stable company, there is a good guarantee that you will benefit from your stocks. Diversifying and investing in several companies is a smart choice to safeguard your investment.

- Dividend income: A good number of stock offer investors dividends after specific periods in the financial calendar. Dividends are important because they not only expand your investment portfolio but can be of great help in retirement. Dividends refer to the income that is derived from stocks that have been sold at a profit.

- Easy liquidity: Shares and securities are often traded in great volumes. Because of this, the market becomes volatile and therefore, as an investor you are assured of easy liquidity. This means that it's simple to convert your investment into cash in order to make better investment choices or use it for emergencies.

- Flexibility: The stock market is considered to be flexible because investors have the power and choice to quickly make decisions. Stocks have their own ups and downs with fluctuating prices at trading sessions. Furthermore, stock prices move in tandem with rapidity of the market.

- Handsome returns: Stocks are considered a risky return because at times, you may make losses. However, in the long term, they offer handsome financially benefits especially if you invested in a company that is performing well and growing on an annual basis.

- Taxation Benefits: Shares give investors incredible tax benefits. You don't need to declare your earnings whenever you are investing in the stock market. Secondly, you only need to report your gains when you make profit from selling stocks. Tax is only paid at the end of the year if you have your earnings in an investment account that earns interest.

In order to become a successful stock trader, it is important to study the gains of investing in the stock market. Seeking expertise advice especially when it comes to making the right stock investment choices is the best thing to do. Your goal should be make more profits without too many risks on your investment.

**Why Would I Choose Stocks?**

For some years, the stock market is an ideal choice for many investors looking for an opportunity to expand their financial fortunes. Before investing in the stock market, it is important to have a reason or reasons why you would want to put your money in stocks. Below are a few of the reasons why people choose to invest in stocks.

- **Retirement**

A lot of people decide to invest in stocks because of the purposes of retirement. A time comes when you are out of a job but require an investment that you can lean back on. For those who wish to invest in stocks to build a retirement fund, it is good to begin when you're still young. Beginning early is a fantastic way to grow your savings because you will not be worried about short term failures.

This is important because it helps balance off the risks that come with stocks because you have a long time to recover and win. Young investors are able to tolerate risks better because the stakes are not high. When you are young, you're more courageous and therefore, you can comfortably invest in risky ventures because you still have plenty of time to build a steady income source. Long term investment is the best approach to build and steadily expand your investment portfolio.

Investing when you are young not only shields you from immediate risks that occur in the near future but enables you to accumulate a huge amount of stocks by the time you retire. While beginning to invest in stocks early is a good idea, this doesn't mean that older people cannot benefit from stock investing. There is certainly nothing wrong investing in the stock market when you are old.

- **Career**

Some people choose to invest in stocks to begin and build a steady career. You don't need to wait till you have retired to enjoy the benefits of your hard work. Today, there are several investors who rely on stocks to make a living. These investors are commonly known as 'day traders' who deal with buying and selling of stocks on a daily basis. These professional traders engage in several transactions and live off the daily fluctuations of stock markets. These types of traders engage in this business for long term purposes and stick to industry despite several challenges. A lot of people have become successfully and substantially expanded their financial fortunes thanks to day trading.

- **Fun**

Aside from retirement saving and day trading, some individuals choose to invest in stocks just to have fun. In most cases, these types of investors are not so keen on making huge profits but rather, have a passion for stocks and want to be part of the industry. However, in as much as they are doing it for fun, they are always keen to keep an eye on companies they've invested in to be sure that their investments are safe.

Regardless of the reason you have, investing in the stock market is one of the best decisions you can ever make.

## How Old Do You Have to Be to Buy Stocks?

What is the right time to buy stocks? This is a question that many people ask. It's important to note that stock investing doesn't have age limitations so long as you have done your research and you know what you want to achieve. Ideally, anyone above the age of 18 is allowed to purchase stocks and become part of the stock market. However, the age at which one decides to invest in stocks depends on a number of factors.

First and foremost, you need to ask yourself whether you are financially prepared to invest in the stock market. As a beginner in the stock market, it is essential to have extra money that you can use to invest. Ideally, the money used for investment should not be part of your daily or monthly expenditures but should rather be drawn from savings. For young investors with big dreams, stock investing provides a good platform for short, medium and long term investment. If you have money to invest in stocks when you're still young, nothing should stop you from pursuing your dreams.

## What are your goals for investing?

Everyone has a personal goal which dictates the level and type of investment. Remember that your investment goals in most cases will not be suitable for everyone. Young people planning to invest in stocks do so because of various reasons. The most common reasons include; seeking additional income, day trading, improve financial prospects and save for assets such as a house or a car.

The age at which one decides to buy stocks is determined by the investment timeframe. As an investor, you need to know what you want to achieve in the future and how long it will take you to do this. For instance, if you intend to purchase a house a few years down the line, you might be forced to purchase stocks when you are still young to allow plenty of time to build your investment.

One should only invest in stocks when they are fully aware about the risks involved. Sometimes, people tend to use stock investment as a quick way of getting rich, this is not true. The ideal age to buy stocks is at a time where you are mature enough to understand the risks associated with stock trading and determine your level of risk tolerance. Remember that investing comes with risks and you need to know that if you're not careful, chances are high you'll end up blowing your entire investment.

How much time are you willing to spare? Just like any other investment, the stock market requires close monitoring if you want to achieve financial gains. Different events and situations affect stock prices which presents an opportunity to transact and increase your investment. If you are keen on trading stocks, the age at which you decide to invest should allow you to have some free time to keep an eye on your investment.

There is no specific age of investing, the above factors act as a guidance on the best time to begin investing in the stock market.

**What are the Main Types of Stocks?**

The stock market is a wide sector and involves several branches. Before deciding to invest in this industry, it is good to know the different types of stocks. As an investor, it is your responsibility to be aware of what happens in the stock markets in order to determine what stocks are best suited for your investment goals. Some companies have devised ways of having stock classes in order to make it easier for investors to choose the most suitable stocks. At the same time, classifying stocks is a technique that some firms use to make sure they remain in control of the largest shareholding of the company.

It's worth mentioning that stocks are categorized into two main groups; common stocks and preferred stocks.

**Types of Stocks**

Large, Mid and Small Cap Stocks: Companies use their market capitalization values to determine how to classify their stocks. In lay man's terms, market capitalization simply refers to the value of a company. In most companies, shares are divided into large cap, mid cap and small cap. Large cap stocks are those with a high value, mid cap stocks are classified as mid-range stocks while small cap stocks have the lowest value. In simple terms, the larger the cap size, the more stable and established a firm is and therefore, the stock price is expected to be stable. On the other hand small and mid-cap companies are focused on future expansion and therefore, chances are high that their stock prices will fluctuate.

**Sector Stocks:** There are stocks that are often categorized into various groups depending on the company's line of business. The most common classification sectors include healthcare, technology, energy, transportation, financial, communication services and capital goods. The mentioned industries are categorized as cyclic in nature while utilities and consumer products are referred to as defensive sectors.

**Cyclic stocks:** These are stocks whose performance depends on the business cycle. The prices for these stocks usually fluctuate depending on the market demand. Cyclical firms manufacture goods or offer services whose demand reduces during tough economic times and financial downturns whereas prices go up when the demand rises.

**Defensive Stocks:** Opposite of cyclical stocks and are known to perform well in the midst of poor economic periods. These stocks are offered by firms whose services and products are in steady demand and enjoy good returns regardless of the state of the economy. Defensive stocks are known to be stable and therefore, still perform well regardless of the prevailing conditions.

**Tracking Stocks:** These stocks depend on the performance of a company's subsidiary and therefore, their results are based on how a company sub-sector performs as opposed to the entire organization. It's worth mentioning that tracking stocks don't entitle shareholders to voting rights. Companies resort to have a tracking stock whenever they feel that a sector which is performing well within the firm has not been fully explored for the benefit of the entire business.

In order to make good decisions, it is important to understand the difference between a common stock and preferred stock as well as their sub categories.

**Where Do I Buy Stocks?**

Today, investing in stocks has become common especially for people who are looking to diversify their investments. Before beginning the process of purchasing stocks, it is important to use a licensed stockbroker. Stockbrokers play a critical role because they act as a bridge between an investor and the company. When choosing stockbrokers, it is good have an idea of where to go. There are different types of stockbrokers that you can go to when you want to buy stocks. They range from cheap stockbrokers who provide simple services to more expensive providers who offer clients a full service that includes in-depth financial analysis, recommendations as well as advice.

Thanks to the internet, investors can now make use of the services of an online broker. For many prospective stock market investors, this is a convenient way to set up an account because you can do it remotely and at a pocket friendly price. Having an account with an online broker enables you to accomplish many tasks with only a few clicks. Online brokers offer basic services that don't include any investment advice and recommendations. If you opt for this broker, you should be ready to make your own independent decisions. The only assistance offered for clients is technical support service for the internet based trading system. If you believe you have sufficient knowledge to comfortably manage your own investments, this is a perfect option.

Discount brokers on the other hand operate similarly to online brokers but they charge a small fee for extra services. If you are looking for somewhere to buy stocks, discount brokers for a small extra fee will guide you with basic investment information. Using this information, they will enable you to make wise investment decisions but will not offer comprehensive analysis and recommendations. They are known for offering in-house research or availing newsletters with investment tips.

Full-service brokers are traditional stockbrokers who dedicate their time to know you personally and financially. A number of factors such as personality, age, income, assets, lifestyle, risk tolerance, debts and marital status are used determine the type of stocks you need to invest in. full-service brokers come up with a customized investment plan that will specifically cater for your needs and ensure your investment goals and objectives are realized. Full-service brokers deal with tax planning, budgeting, retirement planning, and estate planning among other financially oriented services. If you are looking for somewhere to buy stocks where you can get full package advice, this is the best option to go for. In terms of service fees, they're more costly than discount brokers but their comprehensive financial advice and service is worth the additional costs.

Before embarking on the process of looking for a place to find and buy stocks, it is important to ensure that you have researched adequately and made comparisons. Remember, different brokers have varied fees and service agreements and having this in mind while looking for a place to purchase stocks will enable good decision making.

**When is the Best Time to Invest?**

For any investment to take place, you need to make sure that you have researched and made adequate plans. When you try to look for information about how to invest in the stock market, you will realize that there is no specific and accurate answer. However, there is a right time to invest in the right stock in order to make good returns. As an investor, your aim should be to learn how to identify the right stock and do proper investment timing. One strategy to use is to invest in undervalued stocks with great future financial prospects.

Timing is a very important factor when making investment decisions. As an investor, you don't want to lose your hard earned money because of poor investment decisions. Corporate economic growth is usually signified by the high rate of investments. It is vital for investors to learn how to observe market trends in order to determine the appropriate time to make an investment. The stock market is considered across the globe to be highly lucrative and many people have shown an interest to be part of it. However, some investors fail to realize that it's not only about having the money to invest but knowing the right time to invest.

In order to determine the right time to invest, you need to learn more about the industry. Fortunately, there are plenty of information sources where you can find valuable information about the stock market. Reading of journals and magazines is a good way to know what is happening in the stock market industry. By doing this, you are then able to build more confidence in the market and learn how to manage your fears. Different companies go through different financial phases that could present a good opportunity to invest.

For instance, there are some investors who prefer to purchase stocks from companies that are joining the stock market for the first time. In most cases, initial public offers are usually introduced to the market at a lower price to entice investors to purchase. Finding and talking to a professional stockbroker will also give you a good idea when to invest. Stock brokers are the best placed experts to offer information and guidance about the right time to invest in stocks because they constantly keep an eye on the markets. Furthermore, they are the mediator between shareholders and a company and therefore, have access to accurate information.

When you deal with a qualified stock broker, they are always in a position to guide you about the right time to invest. In the stock market, they say every time is investment time but consulting with experts is the best way to keep your risks low. Experts have the capability to analyze the present and future and advise on when and how you should begin your stock investment. Before choosing a particular time to invest, make sure you have done your research and talked to experts before making any financial commitments.

# Chapter Two
# Types of Stocks

## What Are Penny Stocks?

Most of us have heard a lot of folks talk about penny stocks and how investing in them brings huge returns. If you are interested in investing in penny stocks, you need to understand what stocks are and how to invest in them wisely.

Introduction to Penny Stocks

Penny stocks are described as stocks that trade under $1 but this is not the true definition of a penny stock. They are trading stocks on the stock market and the biggest difference between penny stocks and blue chip company stocks is the price. Penny stocks are share prices for small firms, mining companies and startup companies. The price per share in smaller companies is low compared to multinational companies.

Do Penny Stocks have any Benefits?

After learning and understanding what penny stocks are all about, the next step is to find out their benefits. If you want to make huge returns through investments, you need to work with percentages and invest in penny stocks that have high chances of gaining in percentages. Investing small amounts of money in penny stocks has a lot of benefits such as making great returns.

Best Way to Invest in Penny Stocks

Many financial experts and stock brokers' advise that investing in penny stocks is the best way to get into the stock investments world. Through penny stock trading, you learn more about stock trading, shares and nuances of stock trading. The best and most affordable way of investing in stocks is spending between 40 to 60 cents.

Tips to Invest in Penny Stocks

- Carry out enough research and proper planning before investing in pink sheet stocks.
- Start with small investments and gradually increase your investment on penny stocks.
- Invest in a company that has a huge average trade volume. Since penny stocks are highly risky, always have an exit plan ready and be ready to stick to that plan all the time.

Advantages of Penny Stocks

- Trading penny stocks is a guide to learning about the stock markets and how they perform.
- It's easy to start penny stock trading because you don't need to put in a lot of investment.
- It is an opportunity to make money in the shortest time possible by investing in these mini stocks.

Do penny stocks have any risk factors?

When it comes to penny stocks investment, it is possible to make huge gains and at the same time, you could lose all your money on these stocks. There are always risks involved in any kind of investment including pink sheet stock investments. If you are interested in trading stocks in a safe way, you need to depend on analytical stock choosers. They are the best stock pickers who anticipate the behavior of the stock market and the main target is cheap stocks.

Although penny stocks offer great profits, they can also be easily manipulated. If you are not cautious in choosing the right stocks, you can easily lose all your money that you had invested. Always try to find the honest and legit small organizations to invest your money.

## What are Common Stocks?

Common stock is a term that is often used in the stock market. A common stock is simply defined as a share that represents ownership in an organization. Investors who purchase common stocks are allowed to participate in elections by voting and selecting a board of directors in accordance to company policies. When you purchase common stocks, you become part of the ownership structure. In case of liquidation, common stocks owners have to wait until preferred shareholders, bondholders and other debtholders have received their full payment. Common stocks have different names, for instance, they are referred to as ordinary shares in the United Kingdom.

As mentioned earlier, common stockholders are always the last to be paid leftover assets in case a firm goes bankrupt. For this reason, common stocks are considered to be riskier compared to preferred or debt shares. However, purchasing common stocks is a good idea because they are known to be good performers and are likely to bring in good yields compared to preferred shares in the long run and therefore, are an ideal choice for many investors.

When you purchase common stocks, as a stock owner, you are entitled to get dividends whenever the company realizes profits. In most cases, these dividends are usually paid on a quarterly basis. However, some companies have put in place their own arrangements for paying dividends. Whenever a company realizes positive growth, the value of common stocks also goes up. When this happens, stocks appreciate in value and therefore, are sold at higher prices. This positive trend is known as appreciation and in common cases, 40% of the stock profit comes from the dividend while the other 60%

comes from an appreciation. Having the right to participate in electing office bearers is a key advantage that gives stock owners a sense of ownership. In other words, the board of directors is directly accountable to the shareholders.

Common stocks are divided into value stocks or growth stocks. You can purchase value stocks at very minimal prices and the profit you get is as a result of dividends. Growth stocks on the other hand can be purchased at higher prices and therefore the chances of obtaining dividends are minimal. A lot of firms rely on growth stocks for reinvestment purposes to boost growth and enhance corporate development. This means that profits obtained from growth stocks come from appreciation.

Market capitalization is a term commonly associated with common stocks. Market capitalization refers to the price of each stock multiplied by the number of common stocks. This is a standardized index that is used to determine the value of an organization. For instance, companies with less than $2 billion market capitalization are deemed to be small companies. Mid-sized companies have a market capitalization of $2-$10 billion. Large companies are associated with a large market capitalization. When purchasing common stocks, you should always consider the size of a company. This is because investing in smaller firms is always considered to be riskier that dealing with large firms.

### What are Preferred Stocks?

Unlike common stocks, preferred stocks don't give shareholders a right to vote. Preferred stocks are also known as preference shares. For preferred stocks, the investor and company offering the stocks have to negotiate the terms. It's good to mention that preferred stocks can be converted into common stocks. In the case of bankruptcy, owners of preferred stocks are always given priority with payments before other common shareholders.

For an investor who is not too aggressive, preferred stocks are an ideal choice. One advantage of these stocks is that when dividends are paid in a year, the amount due is carried forward and accumulates year after year. When it comes to dividend value, it may or may not remain static. When agreed upon, they can have appropriate par or liquidation value. Preferred stocks can be classified both as a bond or equity. Interestingly, these stocks are classified as equity, they share similar characteristics with debt and are thus considered to be long term investment. Preferred stocks also carry a fixed rate of dividend as opposed to common shares whose dividend rates vary.

Preference shares can either be cumulative or non-cumulative. Cumulative preference shares are where dividends that are not paid within the year are carried forward to the next year. These shares guarantee shareholders a steady dividend stream and therefore, are very popular among investors. On the other hand, non-cumulative preference shares are non-committal because there is no guarantee that dividends not paid during the year will be pushed to the following year.

It's worth mentioning that preference shares can be converted into common equity in the future. A lot of investors who want to avoid high risk shares prefer them because once an individual is sure that a company they have invested in will perform well, they can convert the shares and benefit from capital and dividends stock. Preference shares are a perfect way to protect yourself from current uncertainties in order to benefit from higher stock prices and benefits.

Preference stocks are perfect to be used as business bargaining tools. Some companies have provisions in their charters that stipulate the circumstances under which terms are determined by board of directors at the time of issuance. It's worth mentioning that preference shares are commonly associated with private and semi-autonomous companies. The government reserves the authority to come up with the rules and regulations that determine their issuance. A lot of stock exchange companies are never keen on promoting these stocks.

When choosing to invest in preferred stocks, you need to research widely and be cautious because shares are not equal. A lot of preferred shares are callable meaning in case market interest rates drop, a company can decide to call the shares. When this happens, investors receive their money and the preferred stock is reinvested back into the firm but at lower prevailing rates. Before investing in preferred stocks, it is important to understand their characteristics and determine whether they are an ideal investment choice for you.

### What are Dividend Stocks?

For those who are interested to invest in the stock market, dividend stock is a term that is widely used. The concept of dividends is a common phenomenon in the stock markets that still confuses even those who have already invested in the stock market. A lot of investors receive dividends without knowing where they come from or what their purpose is. In order to appreciate dividends, it is important to understand why they are. Dividends are paid out to shareholders after a company has attained profits from a just ended financial period. Dividend stocks are a portion that is shared by shareholders and often depends on how many shares an individual owns as well as the amount to be divided amongst shareholders.

After the end of a profitable quarter or year, most companies put aside a lump sum which is then divided amongst shareholders. However, it's important to note that dividend stocks are valued at very small amounts because the total number of shares and amount to be divided has to be put into consideration. Individuals who own large shares of stocks get much more than small investors.

So, when are dividend stocks paid?

The frequency of paying dividends varies from one company to another. However, dividends are issued whenever a company realizes a profit. A lot of companies compute their financial results on a quarterly basis and this means that dividend stocks for many companies are likely to be issued on a quarterly basis. There are also some companies that issue dividend stocks more than four times a year while other do it only once in a year. Extended periods of dividend payments indicate that a company could be going through tough financial times. However, when a company chooses to pay dividends in lump-sum, shareholders benefit from a higher per-share payment.

Dividend stocks are rewards to shareholders for a company's good performance. Aside from motivating current investors, dividends are used to lure other investors to buy stocks in companies that pay dividends. When firms receive more investors interested in buying their shares, there is a high chance that stock prices will increase which in turn, will increase a company's profit. Firms that realize high profit margins pay their shareholders higher dividends.

In order to expand your stock investment portfolio, you should ensure that dividend stocks received are reinvested back into the companies that have paid them. This may sound as if you are returning the money back to them but in reality it is a good way of receiving additional stocks in exchange for the dividends. When you do this, chances of receiving higher dividends in the future is high because you own more stocks. This is a smart way of making extra money by ensuring that dividends are put into good use by reinvesting them to have a large stock investment portfolio. Many investors rush to spend dividends on other unimportant issues yet these stocks provide a perfect way to grow your investment. It is only after you have really understood what dividends are that you can effectively benefit from them.

**What is a Cyclical Stock?**

Before investing in the stock market, it is good to understand the different types of stocks and what they mean. Cyclical stocks are issued by companies whose performance varies according to the business cycle. For these types of stocks, the stock prices are high when the industry is performing well and the company is on an upturn. On the other hand, when the company and industry faces a downturn, the prices of stocks also experience a downward trend. Companies in the airline, commodity and white goods manufacturing are designated as companies with cyclical stocks. There are some industry sectors that perform well only during certain seasons and for this reason, stock prices keep changing positions.

Cyclical stocks operate similarly to the wheel of a moving car. At some point in time, a section of the wheel is at the top and as the wheel revolves, the same point that was at the top moves downwards right to the bottom before it begins to ascend again. Cyclical stocks operate using a similar trend; a time comes when they are at the top but after some time, they begin to experience a downward trend, reach the bottom and begin their upward cycle again. Because of the constant repeat in cycles, these stocks are known as cyclical stocks. It's worth mentioning that cyclical stock periods can span over several years.

So, how do you identify cyclical stocks?

These stocks are easy to identify because you simply need to know industries that are always cyclical in nature. Good examples of cyclical industries include airlines, steel and heavy machinery, automobiles, entertainment and travel amongst others. The profits that these companies make always fluctuate depending on the cycle the industry is going through. To be specific, these stock prices depend on the state of the economy and bust cycle. Cyclical stocks flourish on economic booms and suffer major downturns when the economy begins to decline.

Is it safe to invest in cyclical stocks?

This is a question that many potential investors ask. Before putting in money, a lot of people want to know whether these stocks are profitable and if one stands a good chance to recoup profits. This question doesn't have a definite answer because predicting the state of the economy is not an easy task, there is always a lot of uncertainty. Predicting an economy upturn and downturn is never easy. Typically, cyclical stocks perform well when the industry and economy is upbeat. However, stocks remain at low prices for an extended period of time especially due to poor economic performance. In order to make money from cyclical stocks, it is good to master the timing beneficial for buying and selling stocks.

In the event you are planning to invest in cyclical stocks, you need to be fully informed about how these stocks operate. Ideally, you must have a good entry and exit strategy in order to cushion yourself from taking losses. You should know when and how to begin offloading your stocks when the economy begins to lose ground and on the other hand, put in place buying strategies when the economy experiences an upturn. It's important to mention that cyclical stocks are not ideal for investors who are looking for stocks to buy and hold.

## What is a Blue Chip Stock?

When investing in the stock markets, it is important for you as an investor to understand the different types of stocks. Many of you may have come across the term blue chip stock but have no idea what it means or why it is important. There are plenty of Wall Street terminologies and knowing them is the best way to succeed in this business. Blue chip stocks refer to the best stocks in the market and are also referred to as brand stocks. Since blue chip stocks are of the highest quality, chances are high that many investors will have a keen interest to purchase them.

So, how do you identify a blue chip stock?

Identifying a blue chip stock is not as simple as many people may think. One way of finding a blue chip stock is to check the Dow Jones Industrial Average. This is good as it will give you a list of 30 stocks that best fit your requirement and qualifies as a blue chip stock. Actually, the Dow Jones is known as the blue chip index and therefore, you can use it as a trustworthy source to identify blue chip stocks in this index.

However, it's important to mention that being in the top 30 stocks of elite stocks doesn't mean you are safe from risks. It's best to do your research because there are some companies which have exited Dow Jones because of bankruptcy and poor financial performance. Doing your own research and checking for the history of every company is the best way to make investment decisions.

Why should you choose to invest in blue chip stocks? To begin with, many investors are attracted to these stocks because they come with an attractive balance sheet which means more assets and fewer liabilities. A blue chip stock is one that maintains a positive balance sheet and companies owning these stocks focus on corporate growth and development. It's important to note that studying the balance sheet of a company is not a simple exercise and in most cases, requires specialized skills.

Companies with blue chip stocks pay their shareholders' dividends. These stocks move with a similar pattern and rate as S&P 500 which is a collection of 500 stocks that have huge public interest and give an idea of how the entire stock market is performing. Stocks that behave the same or increase with similar rates as S&P 500 are considered to be very safe stocks.

What is the hype about blue chip stocks? There are different types of stocks that you can choose to invest in the stock market. If you don't have time to keep on following how your stocks are performing and require safe investments, blue chips stocks are the best option for you. A lot of people find blue chip stocks to be very convenient especially for long term investment because they can be left alone to grow your investment without putting in so much effort.

# Chapter Three
## Market Orders

### What are some of the Orders I Can Place?

As an investor in stock trading, you are required to execute a position regardless of whether you are trading online or you are using a broker. This is referred to as Execution of an order. Before getting to know about the different types of orders, it is important to understand what an order is. There are various types of orders and selecting them depends on the nature of trade or transaction you wish to carry out. Furthermore, you must put into consideration an analysis of the predictions of how a stock will behave. There are different types of orders but the four most common you are likely to come across are; Market Orders, Limit Orders and Stop Loss Order. However, there are also several other types of orders used in stock markets.

Market Orders: In this case, when you decide to trade a position, you need to get in touch with your broker or use your online trading platform. Once this is done, you can then go ahead and place an order for whatever stock you intend to trade. Here, you have the freedom to choose the stocks you want to trade, their volume as well as price. For online traders, this procedure can be simply completed only with a few clicks.

Limit Orders: With this type of order, you can decide to place a buy or sell order in future after a stock attains a particular price you are comfortable with. This is done after you have carried out a thorough analysis of the stock and have decided the price extent you think it will reach. Immediately the stock attains the expected price, the limit order you put forward activates your account and opens the position for trading. The advantage of a limit order is that if the stock fails to reach your specified price, your order is automatically cancelled. This is convenient because you don't have to spend all your day analyzing trade figures of your stocks.

Stop Loss Order: A stop loss order cushions you as an investor against making huge losses. Smart traders understand that trading with a stop loss order is absolutely critical. For beginners and less experienced traders, this order is vital because it stops you out of position if the prices go too far against what you expected. You need to determine the maximum amount you are willing to lose and put a stop loss at that point.

One Cancels the Other: Commonly known as OCO whereby you can enable both buy and sell positions by placing two orders for the same trade. When the trade attains any of these two positions, the other order you put in place is cancelled. This is a good strategy especially if the stock you're dealing with is experiencing both rising and falling prices and you are unsure which way the trade will go. An OCO allows you to have an option in case of any eventualities.

After Market Order (AMO): This is an option that allows you to place orders beyond the normal working hours for stock markets. It's worth mentioning that all traders who use an online trading account have this feature since online trading transactions can be initiated at any time.

Cover Order: This is a special order that allows a trade an intra-day position and still be able to make use of extra exposure while under the protection of a stop loss order. In this case, a system places both a market order as well as a stop order simultaneously. The corresponding stop loss is only activated after the trigger price is hit and is executed as a market order. A cover entails the simultaneous placement of these two orders and assists you to limit losses that could happen in a particular position.

Before venturing into the stock market, it is wise to research and understand the different types of stock orders and how they can be useful for your trade.

**What is a Market Order?**

In the forex market, there are several terminologies which are usually used. A market order refers to a scenario where a trade has both a buying and selling position. When a trader buys stocks with the hope that prices will increase (trading long), it is said they have entered a trade by buying. On the other hand, when a trader trades short, they have entered a trade by selling and therefore foresee that the price will reduce. Investors make buy and sell decisions based on the current stock market prices. However, in some cases, trades opt not to enter a position using the current prices. The good news is that there are various types of market orders that you can use to enter a position at a price you feel is suitable and comfortable for you. The four main types of market orders are; Buy Stop, Sell Stop, Sell Limit and Buy Limit.

Buy Stop: This is a pending order that a trader uses when they expect stock prices to go up. By doing this, investors have an opportunity to decide an entry price they feel will be safe for them. A buy stop entry is set and once stock prices reach this level, the long entry is triggered.

Sell Stop: The sell stop order operates similarly to a buy order only that in this pending order, a trader expects the price to go down and enter a position at a price he or she is comfortable with. For instance, when trading a USD/JPY pair currently at 100.20, a trader could play safe and instead short the pair to less than 100.20 by setting a sell stop at 99.92. In the event that the price falls below 99.92, the sell entry is automatically triggered.

Sell Limit: Just like stop orders, limit orders are used to enter the market when stock prices are at a certain level. However, for limit orders, they are commonly used as a profit maximizing strategy. This market order is used by a trader when he wants to join the market once the price has enough support and is able to quickly bounce back and continue on an upward trend.

Buy Limit: Buy limit shares a similar concept to Sell limit. In this case, a trader is responsible for setting the price level at which he wants to enter on a given pair. For instance for a buy limit order of 1.2820, a trader could enter and hope for the price to rise to let's say 1.2860 which will represent a 40 points profit.

In summary, stop and limit orders are both used to enter the market when prices are at certain levels and can appear after a period of time when a trader is not physically present and using their computer. Knowing how to best use these market orders is the best way to ensure that you use smart trading tactics that will enable you to make good profits from stock trading.

### What is a Limit Order?

A limit Order is a term that is commonly used in stock market trading. Just as the name suggests, a limit is a restriction order. For instance, when the selling price of a stock gets to a limit that you feel is adequate for you, you can execute the transaction. Limit orders are accomplished when the expected price to transact is attained. Interestingly, a lot of traders are always hesitant to use limit orders when they begin trading. This is because why would you place limits and close trade on a transaction that is appreciating and going in the direction you were anticipating? Wouldn't you prefer to stay on a little longer and obtain the highest profit out of the transaction?

However, limit orders are considered important because not using them exposes you as an investor since you will not get a chance to close the trade. You will also not be in a good position to set targets and know how far you are willing to go with each transaction. In the stock market industry, waiting is risky because a sudden reversal of your expectations could see all your gains erased and losses obtained. Having a limit order enables you to have an approach where you can know if you are nearing a trade and how it will be executed.

How does one set limit orders? This is best done by carrying out thorough research especially about the past history of a stock. Using this information, you can determine the best time and opportunity to place a limit buy. Testing your techniques using a simulated demo account is a good way to learn as well as know the benefits of using limit orders. Testing is important and investors are encouraged to familiarize themselves with how limit orders work before using them in a real scenario.

Working with limit orders improves efficiency and makes work easier. Once you have your limit order set up, you can be able to comfortably go about your activities. By doing this, you don't need to monitor every fluctuation in stock prices. Furthermore, it lowers pressure and ensures that you don't panic unnecessarily and make bad decisions that will compromise your investment. When you effectively use a limit order, chances are high that you will have a rewarding experience because you specify the amount you want the transaction to close at. Using this trading rule that shouldn't be violated also encourages discipline and cushions you against unpleasant experiences of suffering huge losses.

For those buying penny stocks, using limit orders is extremely important because these stocks are known to be highly volatile and therefore, it is important for traders to learn how to cushion themselves. When you put a restrict purchase, it is a positive move because you will have already taken measures to protect yourself. Before investing in stocks, learning what limit orders are and how they can help you to trade comfortably and attain good profits is essential for any trader.

### What is a Stop Loss Order?

When it comes to Forex trading, you will come across the term stop loss orders. What is a Stop Loss Order? How can a trader use them? And how does a seasoned professional use them in trading strategies? A stop loss order is an open order that is started after you have an active order working in the market. A stop loss order lets your broker know when to exit the trade at a predefined level to limit a loss on a trade that has gone against your position.

The difference of regulatory restrictions on brokers in and out of United States requires you to put in a different type of order to complete the same task. This is not a complicated process; all you have to do is to ask your broker to guide you how to set a stop loss on your particular trading platform.

So, how do novice currency traders utilize stop loss orders? The simply determine how much money they are ready to lose on a trade and then set their stop loss at a level that will limit their loss to that amount. However, this is not an ideal way to determine your stop loss point. When it comes to a professional trader, they use a different approach by determining how much money they are ready to lose on a trade depending on their risk tolerance and win or loss system ratio.

However, this is not how they determine where to put their stop order. Professional traders use their system and time frame they are trading on to determine how far they will put a stop loss from the current price. This requires experience and understanding especially on relation to current market price. When the exit point of a losing trade is established, the veteran trader uses the number of pips, their current account balance and their risk parameter to determine what size they need to trade in order to stay within that acceptable risk.

In simple terms, a professional trader adjusts his trade size to stay within his risk parameter. The time frame you decide to trade and the volatility of the currency pair will determine where you put your stop. For instance, a 200-pip stop loss and a 40-pip stop loss is equal in monetary value.

When it comes to trading, a stop loss order should not be used to manage risk but should be used to exit a losing trade at a predetermined price. Using fixed number of pips is not a profitable method to choose a stop loss level. Instead, one should determine where the stop should be in relation to the market and time frame you are trading. One can also determine the size they should trade in order to keep their risk at an acceptable level. Stop loss orders can be placed on a percentage move forward on actual amount. These orders are beneficial because they limit your losses depending on when they were placed.

## What is a Cover Order?

A cover order is an order type the gives traders the chance to place both main order and stop loss order at the same time. This saves a lot of time which is spent in placing separate orders. For instance, if you want to place a buy market order and the maximum loss that one is ready to take is 5%, then you could use a cover order to place the market order with a 5% built in stop loss.

A cover order is a facility that enables people to trade in futures market with minimum margin of even less than 1%. When it comes to taking intraday cover order, traders are also expected to place a stop loss order. The difference required is lot size or quantity multiplied by two times of the difference between buy or sale and stop loss price which is decided by clients as per their requirements. A trader has an option to exit the position before the stop loss is triggered.

When dealing with a stable market, a trader doesn't need to exit from the position and if stop loss is triggered, all the cover orders positions are automatically squared off. All cover orders are executed at the current market price only and limit orders are not allowed.  A cover order facility can be made available by selecting future contracts as per liquidity.

Many trading companies stop loss price or order cannot be modified from any admin terminal or branch.  On the other hand, a client cannot convert or carry the cover order position after giving addition margin. In this case, the trader is required to exit from their current cover position and take a fresh position.

A cover order facility is also a subject to market conditions. This means that if a market is volatile on a specific day, the company can stop the cover order facility for that day. This facility is made available for both offline and online traders. The company a trader uses to trade is not whatsoever responsible if the cover order is squared off at a lower price than the set stop loss price.

One of the benefits of buying a cover limit order is that one can be leave their short position at a price that is lower than the current market price and they can be able to set a minimum amount they are willing to exit. Buy to cover limit orders are amazing for taking profit on short positions. However, if the stock price is reaches the limit price but changes direction to the upside prior your order is filled, a client cannot exit the trade. Moreover, if the price doesn't reach a client's limit price, they will be stuck with their short position.

When it comes to cover orders, there are a lot of benefits which include limited risk and maximum profits among others. Since cover orders work in inherent ways, they assist traders to minimize downside risks and offer better control over risk management. With the presence of a stop loss at each trade, cover orders help users to trade in a more disciplined manner.

**What is an After Market Order?**

Stock market trading or investing may not be a primary profession for many people but it presents a great way to make extra money. Nowadays, many companies offer After Market Offer (AMO) features. This gives traders an opportunity to place an order beyond regular trading hours. This feature is provided to all customers who hold trading accounts.

After Market Order (AMO) is all about trading after market hours and allows a customer to place a stock past market hours. For instance, when regular or normal trading hours closes, news are announced in a company and leads people to invest in the company. During this time, you want to be amongst the first people to invest and not lose out on this opportunity. In this case, you can be amongst the After Market Order for the next trading day.

The use of AMO comes with a lot of benefits that customers stand to enjoy. One of the main benefits of After Market Order is being able to place orders without having to wait for the market to open. One is able to trade and at the same time know when prices may fluctuate. After Marker Order is for customers who are busy during market hours but want to participate. In many post market hours trading, a customer cannot actively track the price movements of stock during market hours. It is possible for one to place an order when they are free after carrying out enough research before the market opens the following trading day. When using AMO, the presence of a trader is not needed at the exchange to execute the order.

Learning how to use After Market Order is simple and fast. A customer needs to log into their trading account and choose the AMO option followed by placing their order. Many companies that offer stock trading are usually open in morning and early nights (7am to 10pm). When one places a After Market Order, they have to consider the closing price. However, a customer has to be flexible when choosing a price which is % more or less than the closing price. For instance, if the price of a stock a trader is purchasing is Rs. 100 at the end of the day, they have the option of choosing the price that ranges between Rs. 95 and 105.

Referring to the above example, when dealing with a buy order and it is placed at +/-5% and the share price opens at Rs. 105 your order is executed at Rs. 105. After Market Orders can also be placed through the Call & Trade facility and this service assists customers to contact customer care support further assistance.

**What are Normal Orders?**

When trading in stock markets, it is important to clearly distinguish between the different types of stock orders and how they can be used to execute transactions. A Normal order consists of a limit and an unlimited order.

Unlimited Order

When you place an unlimited order, this order is always possible to execute since you will receive the shares you are interested in buying at the lowest price which is available in the order book. In case the volume entered is larger, the system matches with the second best price on the order book until the entire order is executed. In some cases, there are no sell offers for securities that are not actively traded. When this happens, the unlimited order is retained in the order book until time comes for it to be executed.

Limit order

Limit orders are different from unlimited orders in the sense that they adhere to price limits. When you put forward a normal order with a limit, you are required to specify a price that is comfortable for you to buy a specified number of shares. The system regards all offers available in the order book that don't meet your limit as unlimited orders. However, execution only happens when the prices exceed your limit. The only pitfall of this type of order is that it will not be matched if your limits are below your expectations. It is good to note that you have the responsibility of deciding how you want your orders to be executed.

Having prior of expectations of what you want to achieve is important because it sets the pace for the strategies you will use to ensure successful stock trading. Understanding what normal orders are and how to apply them to your advantage can have a major impact on the outcome of your stock trading.

## Chapter Four
## Board, Stock Indexes and Sectors

### What is the Big Board?

We have all heard of the NYSE (New York Stock Exchange) but did you know that the NYSE located at 11 Wall Street, New York City has a nickname? Big board refers to the NYSE and goes into history as the oldest United States stock exchange. Aside from being the largest in U.S. it also takes the top position globally as the world's largest stock exchange when measured in terms of market capitalization of stocks listed on the exchange. The two buildings that host the NYSE have been accorded the status of National Historic Landmarks to signify the critical role NYSE plays not only in U.S. economy but globally as well.

The NYSE is a major landmark on Wall Street that attracts both local and international tourists coming to New York City. The Big Board performs a number of critical functions which include; securities listings, setting policies, applicant evaluation and overseeing the changeover of member seats. The Big Board started way back in 1792 after a group of brokers meeting under a tree in the center of Manhattan agreed and signed a number of agreements to trade securities.

Unlike newer exchanges which have adopted recent technologies, the Big Board still makes use of a large floor for conducting transactions. It is on this floor that buyers and sellers representatives and brokers congregate and shout out the prices at each other with the core aim of striking deals. The systems used as the Big Board is referred to as the open outcry system whose aim is to ensure fair market pricing. In order to ensure that floor transactions proceed in a smooth manner, the Big Board has employed specialists whose responsibility is to be in charge of buying and selling of specified stocks and to purchase stocks if no one else does.

When compared to other exchanges, the Big Board has put in strict regulations for any companies that list their stocks on this platform. Fully complying with the requirements still doesn't give an assurance to a company that it will be listed by the Big Board. It's worth mentioning that the agreements signed when NYSE originated is called the Buttonwood Agreement having acquired its name in 1863. The Big Board trades from Monday through to Friday with scheduled regular trading times from 9.30 a.m. and 4.00 p.m. EST. However, on weekends, the NYSE remains closed for trading on weekends and public holidays. It's also worth noting that the Big Board was forced to close for four sessions after the catastrophic September 11, 2001 attacks.

For companies willing to trade on the Big Board, there are a set of regulations that need to be adhered to. However, being the oldest stock exchange in the world, there is a lot of competition amongst companies which are interested to list their stocks on the NYSE. The volume of transactions on the Big Board is enormous taking into account this is the largest stock exchange platform in the globe.

**What is the Dow Jones or the DJIA?**
The United States is known for a beehive of activity when it comes to financial markets. The U.S. has three major indexes or market indicators that provide useful information regarding how stock performance. The three indexes are NASDAQ Composite, Standard & Poor's 500 and the Dow Jones Industrial Average. This is the third most popular index in the stock market that is also referred to as DJIA or the Dow. DJIA alongside NASDAQ

Composite and S&P 500 perform the work of a SMIS (Security Market Indicator Series) whose role is to inform the general public about stock market fluctuations. Using Dow Jones, it is possible to know about the fluctuations in the stock market by giving an indication of how these markets perform specifically during the day.

Initially, DJIA was a representation of an average of 12 stocks only. General Electric started off on the 12 stock index and is still part of the DJIA today. Dow Jones was created by Charles Dow, the Wall Street Journal editor and co-founder of Dow Jones & Company. It was Charles Dow's revolutionary idea to come up with an index whose aim was to assist stock traders. Today, DJIA is price weighted and is determined based on prices obtained from 30 large cap US companies with an active trading history.

So, how are the 30 companies that feature on the Dow Jones Index selected? The 30 companies are picked by Wall Street Journal editors and changes are made based on the current market conditions. Interestingly, 28 companies listed on the DJIA 30 companies trade on the New York Stock Exchange (NYSE). Some of the companies include Walt Disney Co. Johnson & Johnson and General Motors Corp. among others.

Fortunately, it is simple and easy to understand the computation for Dow Jones Average. The total prices of all the 30 companies used in the Dow Jones Industrial Average are divided by the DJIA divisor. The role of the divisor is to ensure the index remains constant in case of any structural changes that happen in any of the 30 listed companies. In the earlier times, computing the DJIA was simpler because the prices of the 30 stocks were used to compute the average. However, any structural changes to firms cause changes to the divisor.

As much as the DJIA has contributed a lot to providing market information, critics believe the average fails to provide an accurate representation of the economy because it only takes into account 30 companies. It's worth mentioning that the DJIA is a price-weighted average and therefore, the average can be affected easily by stocks which are highly priced. When this happens, the public and investors might miss to have a true understanding of the market. Also, the 30 companies that feature on the Dow Jones begin trading at different times in the morning and this can affect the accuracy of calculations for DJIA. Despite this, the Dow Jones is one of the most popular stock market indexes in the U.S.

**What is NASDAQ?**

NASDAQ is an abbreviation for the National Association of Securities Dealers Automated Quotations. NASDAQ was established on February 8, 1971 and is operated and owned by The NASDAQ Stock Market, Inc. It is important to mention that NASDAQ is today the largest online based trading market infrastructure for American equities. NASDAQ has been in use since 1971 and therefore, is the first electronic trading system in the United States. Millions of investors across the world rely on this stock exchange platform for trading. NASDAQ has been at the forefront of attracting listings from foreign companies and is currently, the fastest growing American stock market in the United States.

The advantage of this exchange is that the volume of shares traded on this platform is higher than any other U.S. exchange. The key index in this exchange is the NASDAQ Composite and since inception, has been used for a long time. The NASDAQ 100 index came into existence alongside NASDAQ 100 Financial Index in 1985. For benchmarking purposes, index tracking is done by NASDAQ 100. From March 1 2007, both small and large companies totaling to 5,100 are now established brands which rely on this electronic market for trading. The system is referred to as the American Financial Market share trade whereby out of every seven corporations, two use the platform. NYSE Type A securities account for 14-15% of the shares traded. On the other hand, Tape C takes up about 45-98% of the total trade volume by these companies. NASDAQ platform makes use of a sliding fee technique that is based on the amount of trading markets executed on the NASDAQ systems. With a high number of transactions executed on this system, the removal fee for liquidity will be lower and this means more friendly additional liquidity rebates. In an online trading system, the competition between the best buying and selling prices is always dominant.

A lot of firms know these Market Makers as lucrative markets and are always more than willing to ensure that capital to their registered stocks is instantly invested. Market Makers also play a role in assisting both short and long term stock trading capabilities. In any typical market, both sellers and buyers need are interested in frequent trading while investors want to retain securities for a longer period of time since they're aware their stocks sell fast.

Quotes are classified into 3 distinct levels. Level I inside quotes is characteristically associated with a higher bid and lower offer. Level II on the other hand gives detailed information about market maker public quotes including data about prospective buyers and sellers alongside the most recent orders. Level III is specifically set aside for market makers and allows facilitates them to execute their orders and have their quotes entered. The investing world has continuously undergone several changes thanks to the recent inclusion of various technologies in various online platforms. In the recent times, NASDAQ has also adopted technologies and remains the most active trading system.

**What is the S&P 500?**

Just like NASDAQ and Dow Jones, the S&P 500 is a stock market index that brings together 500 large cap firms drawn from a variety of industries. Standard & Poor (S&P) is responsible for ownership and maintenance of the index. Standard and Poor is a subsidiary of McGraw-Hill. S&P 500 consists of two larger indices S&P Global 1500 and S&P 1200. It's worth mentioning that the firms listed in the S&P 500 trade in both NASDAQ and NYSE which are both the largest US stock markets. The 500 companies that are listed in S&P are considered to industry leaders and therefore, their stocks are watched closely how they perform on the US stock exchange. Procter & Gamble, Microsoft, AT&T and Exxon Mobile are some of the major companies included in S&P 500.

S&P 500 was introduced on March 4, 1957 in order to expand on the previous S&P 90. In the recent times, advancements in technology has enabled the index to perform exceptionally well by doing calculations and ensuring real-time information dissemination. Since its establishment, the S&P index is used as a reference to predict the future of the markets and the US economy in general. There was a time when DJIA – Dow Jones Industrial Average was the commonly used index for U.S. stocks. However, DJIA only consists of 30 companies and therefore, S&P 500 has an upper-hand because it includes more firms and therefore provides a more accurate and true reflection of the market.

It's important to mention that the firms included in S&P qualify after selection by the S&P Index Committee. A large number of companies in the

S&P index are based in America but there is also a fraction of international firms that widely conduct their trade in the U.S. Going forward, the Index Committee has indicated that only U.S. based firms will be added on the Index. In the S&P 500, the weight of each stock is proportional to its market value and therefore, this index is referred to as a market value weighted index.

In case you want to invest in the S&P 500, there are two ways to do it. First, you can opt to purchase individual shares or buy shares of an ETF (Exchange-traded fund). Standard & Poor's Depository Receipts (SPDRs) is one type of an ETF. SPDR has the highest volume of trading daily average with over 200 million shares traded per day. iShares S&P 500 is another form of ETF which shares similarities with SPDRs but here, all members of the index have an equal number of shares.

S&P 500 is widely referred to as the best and most efficient gauge for those who want timely and reliable information about the U.S. equities market. If you are planning to invest, you need to keep a close eye on this world renowned index. Even though the S&P 500 primarily focuses on large firms trading on the stock market, it is also a good basis on which the entire market can be observed.

**What are Agriculture Stocks?**

Agricultural investment has been performing much better compared to traditional asset such as bonds, cash and stocks in recent years. This fact has been backed up by various fundamentals in agricultural investments. With the world population growing, a lot of experts have predicted a high growth in demand for food. This combined with the decreasing supply of agricultural land, the value of land has gone up more than average over the last few years.

Considering investing in agriculture stocks is one of the best decisions you can ever make. As an investor, you can invest in one of the many agricultural funds available on the market. These agricultural funds provide the investor with an opportunity to take part in lower levels and enjoy the lower risk element of spreading their investment over various crops and locations. Another option to consider in agricultural investment is to get involved in direct investment in agricultural land because it is considered as a low risk asset.  Until the end of time, humans will always need food, fuel and feed.

As an investor, you can choose to purchase agricultural stocks because they will benefit you because they in growth value every day.  If you put aside long-term opportunities that promise to perform well even when the economy is weak, you will have more confidence in purchasing even more such investments.  One of the opportunities that are ideal for young investors is to look for stocks that they can hold on to for many years such as agriculture. Investments in agriculture are extremely simple to understand and don't need a lot of knowledge to be able to pick the right stocks as compared to other categories such as biotechnology or information technology.

Agriculture has always been a stable world economy since its invention. Moreover, agricultural stocks have proved to be more stable and reliable choice that provides consistent growth and income. The advance in farming technology, more refined ways of crop cycling and increased demand of organic foods has made agricultural industry an economy to watch.

Agriculture represents a market for crops such as potatoes, wheat and com as well as livestock. Since they are all finite resources, these commodities hold a significant value and can be found in different large agricultural corporations.

The world population is growing and people still need to eat. Firms contribute to food production in a way that generates value in a way that is going to be profitable. If this wasn't going to be the case, these companies can lose money or go bankrupt thus food production will decline. Over the years, agriculture has proved to be the certainly one of the most profitable endeavor going forward.

When it comes to stock investment, you can never go wrong with agricultural stocks. These stocks guarantee money back and they are not as risky as other types of stocks in different categories. Before investing in agricultural stocks, remember to carry out research to choose the right agricultural companies to invest in.

### What are Insurance Stocks?

An insurance stock is a term that many investors don't understand. In fact, a lot of people get surprised to realize that there is a relationship between stocks and insurance. In case you didn't know, it is indeed possible to buy insurance for your stocks. When you purchase insurance for your stocks, you are able to retain some money you had previously invested in case your stocks crash. For smart investors, having insurance stocks is a wise idea because it cushions you against the high level of uncertainty which could lead to massive losses.

Insurance stocks work using the put option. When you purchase a stock using a put option, you reserve the right to sell off your stock once it attains a certain level on or before the specified date. For instance, if you purchase a stock trading at $50 and decide you need to insurance your stock in case it tumbles. This means that you can purchase the $45 put option for a period of 6 months for $5. In the event that the stock crashes, you can be able to purchase the stock for at least $45 within the next 6 months period.

There are 3 main possible scenarios when you decide to insure your stocks.

The stock appreciates in value: If the stock price appreciates to $70 within the six months, you will have gained a profit and therefore, the put option your purchased will expire worthless. As an investor, you have the option of choosing to purchase another put option if you are still convinced the markets are still shaky or if you prefer to take insurance to safeguard some of the profits you have already obtained.

The stock depreciates slightly or remains constant: If the stock prices remain unchanged, the put option will eventually decide and you have the freedom to decide your next step. This means your option cannot be exercised but you can choose to repurchase the option to reclaim part of your premiums.

The stock crashes: This is the worst scenario that no investor wants to think about. However, when stock prices turn for the worse, it's time to make a quick decision. For instance, if the stock price reduced by half to $25 from the original trading price of $50, a loss of $25 would be in the offing. However, because you purchased the $45 out, you still reserve the right to dispose of the stock at $45.

The above strategy is known as protective put and can cushion you against from losses in case stock prices turn for the worst. The stock industry is known to be highly volatile and choosing to have insurance stocks is the best strategy to ensure that your hard earned investment doesn't go down the drain. It is good for every investor to know that there are ways in which you can safeguard your investment and subsequently, trade comfortably at the stock markets. Understanding the importance of insurance is the first step of keeping your investment secure.

**What are Energy Stocks?**

In the recent times, the number of people investing in the stock market has increased. Driven by the need to diversify investments, a number of investors have turned to stocks as a way to build up their investment portfolios. There are different types of stocks that you can choose to invest in. when choosing stocks, you need to have an idea about the various industries and how they respond to market changes. Energy stocks are considered lucrative by many investors because they belong to listed firms that specialize in energy production and supply. Energy stocks belong to firms that explore and develop oil or gas reserves, drilling of oil and gas or integrated power firms.

To understand energy stocks, it is good to have a good idea of the energy sector and how it contributes to economic development. First and foremost, this sector performs in accordance to the demand and supply channels for worldwide energy. For this reason, energy stocks are known to perform very well when the prices of oil and gas are at their peak. On the other hand, low oil and gas prices lead to stock price drops. In addition, this sector is very sensitive to any changes in political temperature which has always been known to have a huge impact on stock prices.

If you have money for stock investment, investing in energy stocks is not a bad idea especially if the investment is done at a time when the market is performing well. If you are looking to invest in the stock market for a long time, financial experts recommend energy stocks because they can be relied upon in the event of a long term investment. For this reason, energy stocks are fancied by modern investors. Investors are always encouraged to invest in these stocks because it is a good way to assist the country realize economic development and become self-reliant when it comes to energy needs.

According to business analysts, investors who have purchased energy stocks are bound to earn good returns from their investments. This industry has a huge potential for investors who are keen on obtaining good returns. It is often said that those who invest in energy stocks are investing in the stock of the future. Despite the fact that the energy stock market industry is lucrative, it is important to do your own thorough research on various companies before making a decision. Seeking the services of a qualified financial analyst can help you to understand how this industry operates and how you can maximize your gains. For potential investors in energy stocks, it is wise to understand every single company operating in this industry as well as their earliest stages of development. Having sufficient data and background information regarding energy companies listed on the stock market ensures that you don't make the wrong investment choices. When approached with the right strategies, energy stocks are lucrative and have the potential to earn you handsome investment profits.

## What are Bank Stocks?

A bank stock refers to a bank's capital that is split into share values of a certain amount. It is possible to transfer ownership of these stocks and they are generally considered to be personal property. It's worth mentioning that the stock market comprises stocks from different companies. Banks are known to be major stock trading players on the market and therefore, considering investing in bank stocks is a wise choice.

Just like any other stocks, bank stocks go through their own highs and lows. However, before investing, it is important to do thorough research and determine which bank stocks are the right one for you. Core bank products such as loans and other financial factors affect the price of bank stocks. Having prior knowledge of how to maximize gains from bank stocks is the best way to realize a handsome return on your investment. Remember that bank stocks are highly financial oriented and therefore, you might not be able to comprehend some theories and terminologies if you lack a financial background. Enlisting the support of a qualified financial analyst or stock broker can help you to make the right investment choices.

So, what makes bank stocks popular among investors? Every investor willing to put their money in stocks is always on the lookout for lucrative stock options that promise a high return on investment. For those who are looking for stocks that are known to be consistent and provide a healthy income stream, choosing bank stocks is a good decision. For people wishing to venture into stock markets, investing in banks is a good beginning for building a sustainable stock portfolio investment base. The steady cash flow and performance consistency makes bank stocks attractive for any investor.

Banks are known to 'cash cows' since they are mature establishments associated with slow but consistent growth. Investors who purchase bank stocks have the guarantee that they will benefit from dividends thanks to regular cash flow streams. According to top investment analysts, investing in bank stocks is a wise move for those who are interested to reap big from the stock market. However, if you want to beat the market, it is good to research thoroughly and identify the top five biggest banks with impressive stock results. It makes sense to examine past financial performance to gather proof that will qualify a bank as best performing in the stock markets. Every country has the biggest financial movers that boast of impressive stock market performance. These firms should be your first priority when investing in the stock market.

Making the decision to invest your money in stocks should be only be made after all the crucial factors have been taken into consideration. The banking industry is known to be one of the most competitive financial sector industries which in turn, hold good prospects for bank stocks investors. Before investing in bank stocks, you should take time to find out which banks are averaging the highest stock prices and the level of consistency.

## What is a Bull Market?

If you're not a stock investor or you are a beginner, comprehending all the jargon that is used in stock trading can be a difficult thing to do. It's important to note that financial markets and stock prices determine financial trends. Using this information about trends, you should be able to select the best investment and identify profitable trading opportunities. Trends are driven by buyers and sellers who are also known as the bulls and the bears. The bulls refer to buyers while the sellers are referred to as bears.

So, what is a bull market? Investor confidence is associated with a bull market and because of this confidence, investors get the urge to purchase more stocks in anticipation of price increases and ultimately, make capital gains. It's worth mentioning that the most memorable and elaborate bull market was witnessed in the 1990s. It is at this point that not only the U.S. but other global markets realized the fastest growth. In a bull market, investors are always making purchases because on the interest to increase their capital gains. The bullish market is associated with investors who are optimistic and are keen on acquiring more stocks in order to increase their profits. A bull stock market is created when there is a significant and steady increase in stock prices over a prolonged timeframe.

For a market to be described as a bull market, there needs to have been a noticeable increase in the price of stocks trading on the market. A lot of investors gain interest in a bull market because they want to expand their investment portfolios. Seeking better investment opportunities is a major undertaking for every investor because at the end of the day, you are keen on maximizing your profits. On the other hand, in a bear stock market, investors are quickly selling off their stocks in order to cut down on their losses. Just to mention, the U.S. is known to be a bull market and it is for this reason why many investors consider U.S. a lucrative investment destination.

Understanding whether you are investing in a bull market is bear market is important because it will determine the kind of decisions that you will take. Without understanding the nature of markets before investing, chances of making the wrong decisions which could cost you an entire investment are very high. It is better to consult with experts in order to understand a bull market, how you can invest and reap profits.

**What is a Bear Market?**

A bear market is described as one where securities prices keep going down and widespread pessimism causes a lot of market negativity which keeps stock prices low. In a bear market, investors anticipate losses because stock markets perform way below expectations of the public. It's important to mention that a bear market shouldn't be confused with short term trends which only last a short period of time. While investors can keenly observe short term trends and use them to enter the market, bear markets are quite challenging to find an entry point because timing the bottom is a difficult task to achieve. Fighting back is not advisable because it is quite challenging for an investor to achieve stellar gains in a bear market not unless one is a short seller.

A common question that investors ask is 'how do I identify a bear market?' The process of knowing how to survive in bear markets is an art and scientific. It is important for you as investor to first and foremost, learn how to identify a bear market. It is said that when 80% of all stocks experience continuous depreciation over an extended time period, this scenario qualifies as a bear market. On the other hand, a bear market exists if major market indexes such as S&P 500 and Dow Jones Industrial Average drop by at least 15%. It's however important to mention that not all sectors experience a bear market at the same time, it depends on a lot of factors. One of the most famous bear markets in the U.S. equity markets took place from 1929 to 1933.

Bear markers have different characteristics and causes. However, experts agree that both investor sentiment and economic cycles are the two major factors that play a role in determining the presence of bear markets. For instance, an economy that is weakening because of unemployment, declining business profits and less disposable income can usher in a bear market. The presence of a couple of trading lows for highly reputable companies might signify the onset of a bear market. When the government gets involved in economic issues such as making changes to federal fund rates and adjusting tax rates, this can also cause a bear market.

A reduction in investor confidence is one of the biggest economic indicators of a bear market. When investors begin to suspect that some events are going to negatively affect their investment are about to happen, they begin selling shares in order to cushion themselves from getting losses. In some cases, the fear of investors to purchase more stocks actually turns into a reality and stock prices begin to decline.

Regardless of where a bear market began and ended, there are four phases. In phase 1, stock prices and investor sentiment is at its peak. Here, investors are keen on maximizing their profits and exiting the market once they've achieved their goals. In Phase 2, stock prices begin to depreciate rapidly, investor confidence and trading activities slump causing investors to panic. When this happens, prices of securities hit new trading lows. In phase 3, the entry of speculators into the market sees a slight increase in stock prices. Finally, in phase 4, stock prices reduce again but this time at a slower pace as speculators begin reacting appropriately to positive indicators. It is known that bear markets often pave way for bull markets.

Bear markets cause investors to lose their earnings because stock prices depreciate across the board. However, the good news is that bear markets don't last forever but they often give no clear notice of their arrival. Smart investors should however have an idea of how to tell if a bear market season is approaching and find ways of maximizing their profits. Because of this, many investors employ market timing tactics to determine when to purchase or sell in order to make good financial gains.

**What is a Market Crash?**

Stock market crash is a term is commonly known within the investment circles but what exactly does it mean? Market crash refers to a scenario whereby there is a sudden decline in stock prices and other securities. It is challenging to determine the exact reason for market crashes but they occur when there is a steep loss percentage. It's worth mentioning that several economic factors contribute to a market crash and a good number of cases have been attributed to investors panicking. In some circumstances, factors such as rapid increase in commodity prices, sudden high cost of living or many positive expectations that trigger a market crash. For instance, when fear causes many investors to suddenly dispose of their stocks, the possibilities of a market crash become evident.

It is for this reason that economic experts insist that negative sentiments have a serious impact on how financial markets perform. At times, these sentiments lead to unforeseen market situations that end up negatively affecting the stock index causing a drastic decline. These drastic and dramatic changes in financial markets performance always affects many people especially those who have directly invested in the securities market. In the recent past, both local and international securities markets have witnessed events that led to a massive market crash. However, it's worth mentioning that the level of severity differs depending on the circumstances that led to the crash.

In 2008, the U.S. had a stock market crash which was attributed to developments in the financial sectors and the housing market. This was a perfect illustration of how market changes which are at times caused by manipulation of various economic factors can adversely affect the financial markets. One cannot deny the fact that market crash is a real scenario that both investors and other industry players have to be prepared for. In the past, a lot of financial markets have crumbled for various reasons and it is impossible to rule out that such scenarios will occur again in the future.

In 1929, the stock market crashed because the central bank had to establish a Federal Reserve and this phenomenon was known as the Great Depression. Since then, the financial markets have in some occasions gone through turbulent times with the September 11, 2001 terrorist attacks causing a stock crash.

If you are keen on investing in stocks, it important for you to begin by understanding what is a market crash and the effects it has on the stock market. When you do this, you can be able to establish your own methodologies of predicting the economic future of stocks you wish to invest in. Market crash is an event that affects not only industry participants but affects investors and the overall economy. The future of many individuals around the world has changed because of market crashes and knowing about them is a good way to learn how to prepare yourself in case of any eventuality. Understanding what a market crash is helps you to be better prepared and identify the signals that call for appropriate action.

## Chapter Five
## Investing Online

### How Can I Open an Online Account?

These days, a lot of investors are gaining interest in the stock markets. With the current changes in technology, trading has become much easier. To participate in the stock market, you need to first come up with an online trading account. These days, many investors prefer online stock trading which can only be done on online platforms. However, you don't need to worry because the process of setting up an online forex account is not difficult. Once you have signed up with a brokerage firm which is required by law, you can embark on the process of setting up an online account.

Before opening an online trading account, it is important to lookout for a broker that has made an effort to simplify their trading platforms. For example, there are a couple of brokerage firms that allow traders to have multiple sets of accounts and their commission charges depend on how much money you have put in your account. Ideally, you should only pay one flat rate for commission regardless of how much money you have in your investment account. However, most stock brokers require investors who have accounts with more funds to pay higher commissions on trades.

If you are a newcomer on the financial market, it's always wise to begin by opening a learner or practice account. To ensure this is possible, you need to make sure that you sign up with a brokerage firm that offers this facility. Using a learner account, you can be able to practice endlessly and in real-time without fearing the risk of losing your money. Fortunately, these types of accounts do not use real money and instead, make use of fake money. This practice is known as paper trading and involves sharpening your trading skills until that time when you are ready to begin participating in real trading sessions. Once you decide to move onto the real account, you need to put in real money and be exposed to the same risks other traders have to grapple with.

Learner accounts mostly have an account maximum while real accounts are likely not to have the provision. It is possible to come across both learner and real accounts that have very low account balance premiums. A lot of online trading accounts can be opened with as little as $50 although experience traders always prefer beginners to start with slightly higher balances. When opening an online trading account, you need to choose an account that you can use to trade multiple securities. In other words, the selected account should not be limiting and should offer technical support as well as expert advisory services.

Of course, before opening an account, make an effort to understand what commissions brokers charge before requesting for an online trading account. In most cases, you only need to have your identification documents at hand in order to set up an account. Since the world has gone digital and everyone is using the internet, opening an online trading account is simple and convenient.

**How to Fund my Online Account?**
Considering the advanced technologies already in place, it makes every sense to use an online trading account to perform your trading transactions. Because of the high levels of convenience, accuracy and security involved, a lot of investors nowadays prefer online trading to manage their investments. However, in order to use an online trading account to execute trades, you need to have money in the account. Fortunately, there are several ways you can fund your online account without having to undergo a lot of unnecessary stress.

Wire Transfer: A lot of people find wire transfer to be one of the most convenient methods of funding an online trading account. The high levels of convenience accompanied by the security and the guarantee that your funds will be reflected in your online trading account in good time has motivated many investors to opt for this technique. It's worth mentioning that when you are using wire transfer, in most cases, the title of your securities equities account and your bank account title need to tally for the transfer to be approved. Wire transfer is a very convenient online trading account funding option especially for traders who wish to transfer huge sums of money into their accounts.

Personal checks: Some individuals opt to use personal checks to fund their online trading accounts. However, it is important to note that this method takes some time because most personal checks have to undergo a 5 business days trading hold period before they're available for withdrawal. This means that it might a little longer before your funds hit your online account. Most brokerage firms require check deposits to be in US dollars and clearance be done through a corresponding US bank.

Electronic transfer: An electronic transfer is a common method that traders use to fund their accounts. However, it is important to mention that there is no specific time within which an electronic transfer takes place because it depends on your financial institution. Broker to broker transfers sometimes take 7-10 days to complete while transfers between banks and mutual fund companies can last anything between 2-4 weeks. Before initiating an electronic transfer, try to find out how long it will take to clear.

Credit cards: A lot of investors rely on their credit card to carry out a lot of online transactions. If you are looking for a quick, stress free and convenient way of transferring money, using your credit card is the best option. Brands such as VISA, MASTER CARD and others allow electronic money transfer and payments.

In light of this, there are several ways that you can use to fund your online trading account. It is important to make sure that you select a method that is convenient for you and suits your preferences. Furthermore, before funding your online trading account, consult with your provider to get information about funding methods which are permitted. Also, it is good to know bank charges and other related transfer charges so that you choose a method that is not only convenient but cheaper for you.

**Do I Need to be a Computer Expert?**

These days, a lot of people are considering the possibility of investing in the financial markets to build their investment portfolios. However, in the past few years, a lot has changed especially with the onset of technology which has revolutionized the entire industry. Nowadays, stock trading transactions have moved from the traditional trading floors to technology compliant channels which are preferred because of their accuracy, speed, reliability and convenience. Given the fact that financial trading is now reliant on the internet and computers, you need to possess a good amount of computer knowledge to successfully execute your trades.

However, the good news is that you don't need to worry if you're not a computer guru because it is easy to learn how to use technology platforms for the purposes of stock trading. A lot of online trading concepts have been simplified to use user friendly interfaces in order to make it easier for aspiring traders to learn the ropes of trading. Fortunately, if you are not a computer expert, there are several trading systems that provide a practicing facility. This means that if you are a novice, you can first begin with an online practice account and learn useful skills that will assist you with trading. Furthermore, there are several software applications that support various trading functions making it easier for traders to better understand the trading environment.

So, what do you really need to know about computers to trade on the financial markets? It's really easy because all you need to have are basic computer skills alongside relevant training especially for platforms you make use of to facilitate your trading. Given the fact that stock trading now relies on the use of computers, there is need for prospective investors to first re-evaluate their level of computer skills before beginning to trade. In as much as you don't need to be a computer guru to become a securities investor, you need to possess a considerably good amount of computer knowledge that can enable you to understand and carry out basic tasks such as navigating stock trading systems.

We are living in the computer age and therefore, it is expected that going forward, the use of computers and the internet will be on the increase. Of late, a lot of stock trading software providers have customized their applications to work with mobile platforms which is a clear indication that the computer based trading systems are here to stay.

**How Can I Overcome my Fear?**

Stock trading is a good investment venture with great financial prospects. However, a lot of investors have failed to fully realize the benefits of stock trading because of fear. Many investors make the mistake of trying to trade while trying to suppress their fears. Always fearing that you will make a mistake every time you do something will always prevent you from moving forward and growing your investment portfolio. In order to make it as a stock trader, you must learn how to overcome your fears.

The following are some ways that you can use to overcome fear;

Work with experienced brokers: It is always cheaper to work with a less experienced professional because it's simpler to pay for their services. However, the risk of facing unpredicted problems is high and therefore, you will always be consumed with fear especially if you have put a lot of money into your investment.

Take time to practice: Before beginning real transactions, it is wise to take time and practice using different platforms. Using practice accounts is the best way to acquire crucial trading skills and gain experience before embarking on real transactions. Through practice sessions, you can be able to learn how to maneuver the market as well as quickly identify factors that could positively or negatively affect your investment. When you know you are not losing real cash, it gives you time to study your trading patterns as well as get to know the implications of taking certain decisions.

Be aware of what you are doing: You can greatly reduce fear if you have confidence in yourself and you understand perfectly what you are doing. You should never put your money in a company whose history, owners and goals you are not aware of. The current and future prospects of a company hold a lot of clues regarding a company's performance. Fear comes in when you make decisions you are not sure of. The best way to overcome fear is to ensure that you access and use information which is accurate from reputable resources. Going through various companies and checking for their respective financial reviews is a good way of making sure you're making the right decisions.

If you are keen on reducing your anxiety and stress levels, make sure to start off on a careful note, make the right choices and remain open minded. With the right approach, you are likely to have fewer problems which in turn mean a less stressful and anxious stock trading experience. You should never get into stock trading with the hope that everything will work out fine, being prepared for any eventualities is the best way to overcome your fears.

Becoming smart and making use of your energy and knowledge before beginning stock trading ensures you make the right decisions. When you begin on a positive note, you ease your fears and ensure you on the track towards becoming a successful trader. The period of making it as a stock trader varies; some achieve success in a short period while others take a longer period. In summary, confidence is the key to overcoming your fears and making it in the stock marketplace.

**What Determines a Stock's Price?**

For everyone who is interested to invest in the stock market, the price of a stock and how it will perform in future in a matter of grave concern. For many investors, a common question that is often asked is what factors determine or affect share price? In most cases, prices of stocks fluctuate because of changes in supply and demand. In the event that many people want to purchase a particular stock, the prices go up. On the other hand, when there are many people interested in selling their stocks, the price dips. In summary, if there is any negative development and traders are interested in selling their stocks, the price will reduce. Before investing in stocks, it is important to understand that there are factors which determine the movement of stocks prices. Below are the most common determinants of stock prices discussed in no particular order.

Bull and Bear Market: Bearish markets always cause stock prices to drop while on the other hand, a bullish market has a positive impact on stock prices because they tend to rise. A good way to understand the direction a market is headed is to keenly observe the index where your stock trading is taking place. By observing the daily averages and volumes of transactions traded, you can have an idea of how the markets are performing.

Company earnings: This is an important factor because traders always invest in a company based on its value and performance capability. If a company does not perform as expected by its shareholders, stock prices tend to depreciate. However, when a firm posts positive results way above expectations, stock prices appreciate.

Events and happenings: At times, there are happenings that occur that were totally unexpected. When this happens, stock prices usually react depending on the event that has happened. For instance, the September 11, 2001 terrorist attacks had a major impact on U.S. stock and financial markets. Other events in this category include natural disasters and political events. Take-overs, acquisitions and mergers: When firms decide to join operations, this decision has an effect on stock prices. In most cases, the company joining the merger witnesses an appreciation in the value of stocks while the company taking over has its stock prices depreciate in value.

Changes in rates: When central banks announce changes in market rates, these changes begin to take an immediate effect on stock prices as investors begin to make appropriate decisions in response to the announcement.

Changes in rates imply that various parameters such as home loan rates change which ultimately affects stock prices.

Performance of the industry: Just like market changes, how an industry performs also has an impact of stock prices particularly in that sector. In most cases, depending how the industry is performing, most stocks in that sector tend to follow a similar trend except in isolated cases where other factors also contribute.

Stock buybacks: When a firm decides to buy back its stocks from shareholders, the price of the stock will appreciate because the demand will be higher. For various reasons, firms opt to buy back stocks from the stock to achieve various corporate obligations.

Company announcements: When a firm makes a major announcement, stocks prices begin to experience fluctuations because traders attempt to make predictions of earnings, industry changes and management changes. On the other hand, when a firm makes an announcement that is not well received by investors, share prices tend to drop.

War and political instability: We are living in a world whose security has become highly volatile and anything can happen. Financial markets are very sensitive and any political instability or war has adverse effects on stock prices.

Dividends: When a company pays out dividends to its shareholders, the stock which is now ex-dividend experiences a price fall by the dividend value which is supposed to be paid out.

Before purchasing stocks with any company, it is important to fully understand what makes stock prices to fluctuate and the decisions that you can take to react to any changes in the market. Wise investors are supposed to be wary of any factors that affect stock prices as this is the only way to safeguard an investment.

## Chapter Six
## General Investment Questions

## What is the Difference between Growth Investors and Value Investors?

In stock investing, there are different terms that are often used to explain various investment concepts. For those of you who are planning to venture into the stock market or are already in this business, you must have heard of a growth stock and value stock. These are common terms used in investing but what exactly do they mean?

It is difficult to come up with a clear and set definition of growth and value stocks. However, there are some criteria that are used to define these stocks.  It's important to mention that growth and value are not only methods of investing but also act as a guide for investors to narrow down their options and know what to invest in. For those who understand the stock market well, you will agree that there are times when growth stocks perform very well and others when value stocks excel. It is a wise investment practice to have stocks in a diversified portfolio in order to cut down on your risks.

Growth investors are those who focus on growth investing that revolves around a stock that has exhibited a potential to grow. On the other hand, value investing focuses on underpriced stocks but still have enough room to increase. Growth stocks are usually associated with strong growth capabilities. Here, investors are keen on having a stronger return on equity. If you are interested in growth investing, you need to take into account both the pre-tax earnings and the earnings per share. Once this has been done, it is wise to project the future stock price in order to have a good idea of how much you are likely to earn.

As a growth investor, you need to be wise and use your judgment and common sense to make wise decisions. It is possible that the stock might currently not meet all the criteria but still has a chance to qualify as a solid growth stock.

Some people think value stocks are cheap stocks which is not the case. However, there are some instances where value stocks are listed alongside the lists of firms that have hit a 52-week low. For investors, value stocks are used as the bargain for investing. The ultimate aim of value investing is to select stocks that are underpriced and wait for the prices to attain their ideal market rates.

How do you identify value stocks? A good way to choose a value stock is to find stocks with a price to earnings growth ratio of less than 1. The price earnings ratio should rank at the bottom 10% of all firms. A good value stock is one whose share price is a tangible value.

There are investors who prefer to focus on one type of stock and ignore the other. This is not a good strategy because diversification of portfolio of both value and growth stocks is the best and guaranteed ticket of obtaining good returns. If you are a beginner, investing in both stocks is a good starting point.

## What is a Speculative Investment?

Speculative investment otherwise known as investment speculation is when an investor purchases a stock or bond with an aim of obtaining a dividend or interest. However, there is also an interest to sell the stock at a better price in case there is an increase in stock price. On the other hand, speculative investment is when an investor purchases a stock that is not yet paying dividends but the investor hopes to start receiving payments in the near future. This is after there is an improvement in the price of the security.

In stock trading, speculation is a common phenomenon as several investors are always attracted to the stock market. Speculation is manifested in several forms in the stock market and is commonly associated with investors who have plenty of disposable income to accommodate a loss. Speculative investment comes in various forms which includes; option trading, futures trading or commodity trading and penny stock trading. Futures or commodity trading is known to be a highly speculative form of stock trading. In option trading, stock options are derivatives that obtain their value from the main stock and as a result, are highly speculative. These stocks can expire without gaining any value after a specific period of time.

Penny stock trading is a common type of speculative investment. A lot of investors prefer putting their money in penny stocks because they are cheap to acquire and can be purchased in bulk amounts for less money as opposed to larger stocks. However, these stocks have a disadvantage because they attract very little activity for several weeks or even months without market makers executing any trades. Firms that deal with penny stocks are traditionally considered to be small corporate entities with little or no cash or shell firms without a viable business plan.

Penny stocks have in the past been associated with fraud with unscrupulous traders who use these thinly traded stocks and sell them to investors as the price increases. However, for those keen on speculation, penny stocks can come from viable companies with sound business plans, great futures but limited financial sources to spur investment. Putting your money in such a company implies you have high chances of making good gains because the stock price can appreciate substantially.

Most investors who engage in speculative investment for penny stocks have limited financial capability and can therefore, not withstand the loss. Because of the attraction to these cheaply priced stocks, speculators in quite a number of cases end up losing their investment. This happens because some investors opt to continue purchasing more stocks as prices tumble with the hope that prices will appreciate and regain previous highs. In some cases, investors fail to realize any substantial gains especially after the stock prices have dipped to low levels. This is however a normal occurrence with speculative stocks.

When investing in these stocks, you should be ready to cope with the rapid changing stock prices. Should you decide to engage in speculative investment, you need to know the best time to act and make quick decisions.

**How do I know I make the right investment?**
One of the important fundamentals when it comes to investment is choosing the right investment. Nowadays, there are many investment options available to you and making the right choices that can support your short and long term financial goals is important. Choosing the right investment depends on your goals and expectations but with the help of some general guidelines, you can be able to aim towards the right investment choice for you.

To know that you make the right investment, you have to make the right decision. First, you have to sit down and go through your overall financial situation. The first, step to successful investment is figuring out your goals and risk on your own or with the help of a financial expert. If you are interested in investment, you need to know there is no guarantee that you will make money from investment. However, if you get the facts and understanding about saving, investment and follow through with a great plan, you can be able to gain financial security and enjoy the benefits of managing your money.

When it comes to investments, there is always some degree of risk. If you plan to buy securities such as bonds, mutual funds or stocks, it's essential that you understand before investing because you could lose money. Unlike deposits such as NCUA insured credit unions, the money that you invest in securities is simply not federally insured. It is possible to lose your principal which is the amount you have invested.

The benefit of taking on risk is the fact that you can have greater investment return. If you have financial goals, you are likely to make more money by carefully investing in asset with greater risk like bonds or stocks rather than investing in assets with less risk like cash equivalents. On the other hand, investing in cash investments can work can be ideal for short-term financial goals. The main concern for individuals investing in cash equivalent is inflation risk.

Considering an appropriate mix of investments is a great idea. These investments such as asset categories move up and down under various market conditions which can protect an investor from losses. Investing in more than one asset category can reduce the risk of an investor losing money and their portfolio overall investment returns.

An investor investing heavily in shares of employer's or individual stocks is recommended to make the right investment. One of the most important methods to reduce the risks of investing is to diversify your investments. Choosing the right group of investment within an asset category can limit your loses and reduce the fluctuations of investment return without letting go of too much potential gain.

Making the right investment requires an investor to create and maintain an emergency fund. A smart investor should put enough money in a savings product to cover for any emergency. Paying of high interest credit card debt is also a great idea. As an investor, you also need to know there is no investment strategy that pays well or offers less risk. If an investor owns money on high interest credit cards, the best thing to do in any market condition is to pay off the balance in full as fast as possible.

An investor also needs to avoid circumstances that can lead to fraud to make the right investment. Nowadays, there are a lot of scam artists being publicized to lure potential investors. Taking enough time to carry out research and ask essential questions is a great way to stay off scams. Many investors have lost their investment by investing in the wrong investment options. To make the right investment decision, you need to allocate extra time to carry out enough research to find the right investment.

## Why Should I Invest in Different Stocks?

Everyone understands the significance of finding suitable ways to invest in order to set aside savings for future use or raise money for various personal or business ventures. The stock market is one of the most common platforms for investment and therefore, many investors are keen to put their money into financial markets with the hope of obtaining good financial gains.

Unfortunately, some investors have no idea of how to invest safely and properly and therefore, end up investing their money in stocks from one sector or company.

In most cases, when purchasing stocks, investors rely on stock brokers and other people such as family and friends for advice. If you are interested in becoming a stock trader, you should research carefully and pick a handful of stocks that appeal to you. This is important because taking into account the volatility of the stock market, you cannot afford to put all your money into one stock. Investors get tempted to put their entire investment in one stock that seems very lucrative because of impressive financial performance. As much as there is a potential for making good profits in the event of stock price rises, there is also a danger of losing your entire investment that you worked so hard for should the stock you purchases take a turn for the worse.

Many people fail to realize that they've invested in one form of stock which is a wrong move until it is too late. Investing in individual stocks is simply a bad idea because you end up putting all your eggs in one basket with a high risk of all of them getting wiped out. When you opt to put all your money in a single investment, chances of losing money are high. However, putting your money in a broad stock market index cushions you against the risk of losing all your money.

When you invest in different stocks, you have a good chance of spreading your risk and therefore you don't have to keep panicking when stocks of one company trade below your expectations. Investing in different companies also has a lot to do with the level of risk tolerance. If you know that you cannot cope with very high levels of risk tolerance, you should avoid placing your entire investment in one stock. It doesn't make sense to put all your money in an investment that will make you worried throughout.

Investing in the stock market index fund is a smart way of cushion yourself against unforeseen risks. The stock market index fund works with the entire stock market and keeps you away from the risk of individual stocks. If you are unsure of which stocks to invest in, you should learn how to get the appropriate information before making any financial commitments. In order to invest securely, look for the best stocks from a range of companies to ensure you spread your investment and still reap the benefits of the stock market.

**What are the best long-term investment strategies?**
When it comes to investments, you have chosen the right investment opportunities to make money. Unfortunately, many people have lost a lot of money because of making investment without carrying out enough research. As an investor, you need to put your hard-earned money in promising investments. Using long-term investment strategies is a great idea to invest your money. So, what are the best long-term investments strategies to use?

Staying in the course through Ups and Downs is one of the best long-term investment strategies. Studies show that the market goes up and down. Although there are short-term losses, the market has a tendency to rebound and reward long-term investing by moving higher. If stay fully invested, you stand to benefit from rebounds. Many long-term investors enjoy the market's power and the ability to stay on the course. When you invest, you need to know that no investment strategy promises a profit because chance of investment returns fluctuating are high. At the back of your mind, you need to be aware that you can lose money in any investment.

Buying right and sitting right is another good long-term investment strategy that an investor can use. In treading, market timing doesn't work. You can never know when the market gain will take place and missing on the best market days can lower your return immensely. To take advantage of market gains, you have to fully stay invested and avoid timing market moves. However, staying fully invested doesn't guarantee any profit.

Learning about market opportunities is also a great long-term strategy that comes in handy. When investing, try as much as possible to keep your emotions in check. According to studies, the market volatility has made investors to make emotional decisions. In this case, investors tend to purchase high and sell low based on emotions rather than choose the proven method of staying in the course. For instance, a lot of investors have gone through large equality inflows in the past years and at the same time, the market has peaked. There are some other cases where large equity outflow occurs and coincides with a market bottom. Of late, large equity outflows takes place just before the market reaches a low point.

Capitalizing on market declines is also a part of the long-term investment strategies. An investor needs to know that bear markets and corrections are normal occurrences happens about often. As a wise investor, you need to be aware that bear markets and corrections can present great buying opportunities. Adding investments after the market drops is a great way to take advantage of lower stock prices, though this doesn't ensure profit.

All in all, an investor needs to use the best long-term investment strategies to make sure they make the most out of their investment. There are so many strategies that one can put in place to make sure they get profit.

## What do stock investors really need?

Nowadays, there are a lot of sources providing investment advice to investors to enable them make the right choose and decision when investing. Although this information has helped investors, the system has not worked. This proves that this information being offered is not what investors need. When reflecting on our experiences as advisers and investors, we need to come up with what we believe is the key to meet the wants and needs of investors. Investors bring conflicts to advisers for them to resolve. If investors want safety and growth and when the markets are volatile, investors want advisers to do something to stabilize the swing in the value of their portfolio.

Investors are in need of adequate pool of investment money in the future and to enjoy using it today. When the stock market is high, investors don't want bonds until the market corrects. This is the reason why investors want equality like returns without the volatility. Many investors want to perform favorably against any selected capital market indexes while making steady increase in purchasing power.

Stock investors want advice that will help them to achieve their goals. These desires can often lead to disappointment and can lead to devastating results. It is our duty of advisers to resolve these conflicts for investors. To create and encourage successful participation, investors and advisers should ask the question, what do investors want? This in turn can enable them to develop investment offering that deliver what they want.

One of the ways to define what investors really need in terms of personal financial goals is to understand their goals. Some of the goals include current income, setting money aside for a rainy day, appreciation in investment value with reduced volatility and long-term growth to fund retirement.

Another way to define what investors want is through the terms of the experience they seek. This can include competitive returns, managed volatility and return per unit risk. This concept can be understood in terms of what investors value such as objectivity, predictable outcomes, managed volatility, income management, communication and transparency. Delivering an investment experience that contain a mix of these elements and fits the investor's personal goal and desires experience, these serves as a personal backbone for investing strategy that should be developed and executed.

Investors always talk about and think about comparing their investment strategy performance to capitalize market indexes to assess their investment experience. The challenge is capital market return and risk is not important for achieving personal goals. Capital market indexes measure speed and risk is not important for achieving personal goals. To define the progress towards goals, there is need for purchasing power. Capital market indexes have return characteristics that tell investors their level of volatility they may encounter.

Since stock market is a risky field that an investor risks losing money, one needs the right information that will teach them the required skills and knowledge required. What stock investors really need continues to be a major question that experts continue to expound on.

**What are the best reasons why I need to invest?**

One of the most compelling reasons why many of us invest is the prospect of not having the need to work our entire life. All in all, there are two major ways to make money; working or having assets work for you. If you keep your money in your saving account instead of investing it, your money does not work for you and you will never have more money than what you save. By investing in your money, you will be making your money to generate more cash by earning interest on what you keep away.

At times, it doesn't matter what you do to make more money. Whether you invest in mutual funds, bonds, futures, options and stocks among others, the objective is to make money in return. To make investment that will generate more money for you in the future. Whether your goal is to purchase a house or go for a trip in the future, investing is important to make your dreams come true.

Many people always wonder what they can do to invest or why they need to invest. There reasons for investing are clear and simple. Investing or investment makes one to prepare for the future. No one wants to work their whole life. Investing is one of the best decisions that one can secure for their future.

One of the main reasons to invest is to keep your money with yourself instead of investing it. If you don't invest, you will only have the money in your account that will increase to cater for your future. It is possible to invest your money and generate more money by earning interest on what you have put aside. People choose different ways of investing which they think will work for them. Some people think that keeping their money in the bank pays them a good interest and wonder why they need to bother to find other ways for investment. Fortunately, not all folks think this way because some people invest their money and gain profits out of it.

If you wish of earning a large sun of honey for your future, you need to invest now. When it comes to investment, it's never too late to invest. The earlier you start your invest, the better and easier it will be for you to build your future. You can find a lot of short, long term and intermediate plans to choose from when it comes to investment. You need to keep these investment plans in your mind when you are thinking about investing. Choosing a great investment plans will enable you to make more money for you.

When it comes to investing, you should not have any second thoughts because you are doing good to your future. There are so many reasons why you need to invest if you care about your future. To be able to enjoy your old age, you need to start investing now to grow your money. When it comes to investing, you will never regret why you did it in the first place.

**Why Should I Invest Regularly?**

We are living in tough financial economic times and it makes sense to plan for your financial future. With the high cost of living, a lot of people are complaining that income earned from employment is hardly enough to cater for all personal and family needs. In the recent times, we have witnessed an increase in the number of people who opt to borrow loans sometimes to even cater for their monthly bills. There is nothing as sweet as being financial independent knowing you have enough money even to guarantee you a comfortable retirement.

With a lot of uncertainties, it is important for you to learn how to invest early enough in order to allow your investment portfolio to grow. Instead of keeping your money in an account, find something useful to do with it and try to see how you can use investments as a way to expand your financial capabilities. Investing regularly is a virtue that anyone who is keen on securing their financial future should do. Nowadays, there are numerous investment opportunities coming up on a daily basis and it's good for everyone to learn how to tap these opportunities for financial gains.

Investing is not a one day affair. In order to be successful, you must learn how to keep your eyes open for any new securities or other forms of investment that avail good opportunities to make money. Remember that you shall not be working your entire life and therefore, you need to start investing early in order to meet your financial goals in life. There are several projects in life that demand a lot of money and investing regularly is the best way to ensure that you continue to gradually accumulate wealth. Financial expenses such as family medical expenses, school fees, family upbringing and retirement funds are the reasons why we need to invest regularly.

For many people, it is impossible to accumulate wealth in a small amount of time unless you have won a lottery. Unless you are in a very lucrative and high paying job, you can never have enough money to cater for both your current and future needs. Unfortunately, many people especially young adults only focus on acquiring money to cater for present financial obligations but forget about the future. Regular investment ensures that your investment portfolio keeps expanding and also prevents you from withdrawing your investments prematurely in order to keep up with a lucrative lifestyle.

Persons who invest regularly understand that financial security is a continuous process that involves looking around and identifying new opportunities you believe will uplift your financial status. There are so many places you can invest and earn a good return on investment. It is important to mention that when investing, you need to ensure that you focus on opportunities that genuinely interest you and match your preferences. Investment is the best way you can plan your finances and watch your financial prospects gradually grow over a period of time.

**What are the Rules in Investing?**

You can only consider yourself to be successful investor if you have adhered to the rules to investing. The nature, technique, type as well as the discipline associated with investing is what makes some people rich and others not.

Rule number one of investment is that you must come up with a sound investment plan. Wise investment dictates that you need to carefully evaluate every opportunity and determine how much growth is there for you. Also, it is important to choose investment that will not cause you management headaches; the investments also need to be safe. Before making any investment, you need to identify what type of investor you are or which group you belong to. This can easily be determined by your age and your stage in life.

For instance, if you are single and below the age of 40, your focus should be on long-term investments aimed at both capital and compound growth. For married couples without children and between the age 20-40 years, long-term investments aimed at increasing capital gain are the best solution. Individuals who are over 40 years are encouraged to go for medium term investments with medium risk with both capital gain and compound growth.

Understanding the types of Investments

You should never go ahead and put your money in a project you do not understand. For starters, there are 3 main types of investment that you can choose from; low, medium and high risk investments.

Low risk investments: This category includes superannuation, fixed interest and cash. Risks are the lowest meaning a less return on investment. Cash management trusts and bonds are examples of low risk investments.

Medium risk investments: Non-speculative shares and property are classified as medium risk profiles. In most cases, mutual funds are also included in this category with annual interest rates of 8% to 25% depending on the type of fund.

High risk investments: Any investment that is speculative in nature is referred to as a high risk investment. For instance, speculative shares are referred to as high risk profiles because investors put their money into these investment projects not knowing whether the prices will go up or down.

Have an investment program: Once you have made a decision, you need to come up with an investment timetable. You can either do this on your own or hire an expert financial advisor to help you with timelines. Doing this is important because you need to know the best time to enter and leave the market. Also, you should have a long term plan of how you intend to invest your money and what you intend to achieve.

Summary of Investment rules

Below are a simple set of rules which if followed will guarantee you a successful investment experience:

1. Have a plan: Make sure that your financial advisor gives you a sound investment plan that takes into account your financial goals, timeframes and risk profile. A lot of people fail to succeed in investment because of taking part in investment projects with a clear plan.

2. Avoid investing in only one venture: The saying 'don't put all your eggs in one basket' sounds rather obvious but unfortunately, is ignored by many investors. Doing this is very dangerous because you risk losing your entire investment should an investment portfolio you have put money in collapse.

3. Build appropriate and realistic timeframes: in order to be a successful investor, you must learn the art of investment timing. You need to know how to react to various investment periods and still make the appropriate decisions.

4. Keep steer of high risk investments: If you know you're not willing to tolerate high risks, then you should stay away from risky business projects especially highly speculative stocks.

5. Don't rely on debt to invest: A lot of financial advisors support gearing your investments. Gearing means borrowing in order to invest. If possible, your investment should come from your own savings as this is the best way to build your financial prospects – away from debt.

Learning how to save and invest from your income is a good habit for anyone who wants to invest successfully.

6. Invest in projects you understand: The best way to stay calm and watch your investment grow is to invest in a venture that you understand both its advantages as well as pitfalls.

**What are the Guides of Choosing a Good Investment?**

Making good investment choices is the only way to achieve financial prosperity. If you have worked so hard for your money, you need to be careful where you put it to avoid uncalled for losses. There are several investment ventures out there and choosing an ideal one is a crucial step. Since you are only bearing the dangers associated with an investment, wise planning is critical. It is important to note that unless you have guaranteed income and enough money to spare, you should avoid going for high risk investments which can leave you penniless in a split second. Before putting your money in any investment, it is important to note the following things;

- There is no secure investment plan because every venture is associated with its own set of risks.

- There is a close association between risks and returns. When the risk is higher, chances of a higher return are evident.

- Never put your money into any investment without first understanding the implications.

- Before investing, you need to set your goals and know what achievements you want to gain after investing. While some investors look for individual goals, others go for investments that offer multiple benefits.

- Evaluate all issues and risks related to the safety of an investment. To be on the safer side, it is always a good idea to go for investment plans with low risk. Even if your returns are reduced, you're always guaranteed that your money is safe.

- Your income is a major consideration because it determines how much money you're willing to put up for investment. For instance, if you are looking for an investment that will give you a regular source of income, you might have to invest more in the beginning.

- Your investment choice should depend on the type of growth you are looking for. If you are keen on growth, choosing a long term investment is wiser. With this type of investment, you are guaranteed of the appreciation in market value.

Whatever choice you make, you need to be careful and avoid putting all your eggs in one basket. By doing this, you are assured that you shall get a return on investment at least from one of your investment ventures. Investing in a single investment venture is a risky affair that has caused investors to lose their hard earned income.

Also, you should never invest your entire money and remain with nothing. Investment is a gamble and you cannot afford to give out all your money including finances set aside for emergency use.

When considering any investment, you need to be final decision maker because at the end of the day, it is your money and you have the final say. Of course, seeking advice from a qualified professional who is licensed is always a wise idea.

Finally, before selecting an investment, you need to make sure that you critically examine a company's background and track record. Taking into account the present successes is not enough. Investment decisions also have to be made after careful scrutiny of information provided. You should never trust or use unsolicited information to make key investment decision because the authenticity of such information is not known.

**What are Common Investment Vehicles?**

If you are planning to invest, you should know that there are different types of investments in the financial market. It is important for prospective investors to be adequately educated for making any decisions. Before putting your money into the financial market, you need to know the available investment vehicles in order to make an informed decision.

Corporate bonds: This is a common investment vehicle especially for investors who are looking for a long term financial investment plan. Compared to government bonds, corporate bonds are known to offer higher returns. However, you should know that there come with a slightly higher risk than government bonds. If you are looking for a safe investment, going for a highly rated corporate bond is a safe investment.

Government Bonds/ Money Market Accounts/ Certificates of Deposit: The advantage here is that they are all less risky and therefore, you can be assured that your investment is safe. However, the unfortunate part is that they offer the least investment. These 3 investment vehicles are ideal for investors who are keen on keeping their investment capital.

Mutual Funds: Mutual funds have the capability to offer very lucrative returns on investment. Unfortunately, the fees involved are too and some mutual funds end up performing dismally than market indexes. High management fees and restrictive trading policies are some of the downsides of mutual funds. When you invest in mutual funds, you cannot buy and sell stocks at any time you wish because you have to comply with the rules of the fund.  With wise selection, they offer a good opportunity for substantially building your investment portfolio.

Stocks: Stock trading is a common investment channel and a favorite for many investors. The ease of becoming a stock investor and less trading restrictions has contributed to the popularity of stock as an investment option. In order to achieve returns, you need to be active and watch the movement of your stocks. The risks of losing your investment are higher with stock trading and therefore, you have to be careful with the types of stock you choose.

Options: On many occasions, not many investors invest in options because they are considered a too risky investment. Options carry a higher risk than stocks and therefore, investment should be done very carefully. It's good to note that options are very lucrative because they can give you as much as 100%-200% per day. However, with a robust and well-designed trading system, it is possible to comfortably trade options without undergoing a lot of risk. So long as you learn how to minimize risk and focus on upward potential, you're definitely headed for very rewarding and handsome gains.

Before choosing any investment vehicle, you need to be careful and avoid making rush decisions. Talking to a reputable and experienced financial advisor is the best way to access accurate information and facts about each type of investment. Make sure you know and study all your options before finally making your investment decisions.

**What Should I do to develop the Right Mindset?**

For you to be successful in whatever you do, you must learn how to develop the right mindset in order to achieve personal growth. It's also worth mentioning that correct mindsets also help you a lot when it comes to personal finance development. The good news is that there are several ways to cultivate the right mindset and you only need to go through them and choose what will work best for you. In order to achieve any personal growth, it takes a lot of self-discipline and dedication to achieve your goals. The process of changing your mindset is not an instant thing. It is a process that needs to be practiced on a daily basis for any tangible results to be achieved. Lack of dedication towards embracing new mindsets means there will no positive changes to your personal growth.

One of the best ways to change your mindset is to identify someone who inspires you. For instance when it comes to finances, you can choose an individual who has performed well in this area and use them as a reference point of what you intend to work towards. One of the best strategies to use is to use latest technology platforms such as social media to connect with them. For instance, you can follow them on twitter or become their fan on Facebook. You can borrow from them on issues such as their lifestyle and set your own goals. It is also a brilliant idea to find someone who can act as your personal coach in order to remain on the right path to success.

If you are keen on adopting the right mindset, you need to stop any thought patterns and bad habits. For instance, you can read a book on changing your mindset and make a commitment to read it every day. Once you are done, you can find another book with a similar topic or read the same book once more just to have a better idea of what having the right mindset means.

Personal growth has to happen on a daily basis. This means that you need ample time every day to reflect on your current life, set goals and think of strategies to use to achieve your goals. You can close your eyes and reflect on the type of future you'd wish to have and what you will be doing next after you have attained your goals. Personal growth can only be achieved if negative habits are replaced with positive traits. It is not easy to let go of a habit you have been practicing for so many years but sacrifice and focus is required for this challenging task. In case of failure, you shouldn't give up but rather use the failure as a stepping stone to work towards your goals.

Having a set of goals and listing them down where you can see them is a constant reminder of what you need to do. Setting goals only is not enough; planning is an essential part of achieving your goals and consistent effort must be taken to shift you closer to your goals.

Changing your mindset requires you to associate with people who are always optimistic and supportive. Individuals who always whine and complain about everything are not good for you because they can easily ruin all your efforts to achieve your goals.

**What is the Difference between Bull Market and Bear Market?**
If you are keen follower of what goes on in the investment market or you're an investor yourself, you must have heard of the terms 'bear' and 'bull' market. Many of us have come across these terms either through the

internet or on business platforms discussing financial markets. Understanding the difference between a bear and bull market is the best way to know what these terminologies mean.

A bear market refers to a period within which a market is on a decline and this term is often commonly associated with the stock market. When stocks experience a steady decline over an extended period of time, the market can be described as bearish. This can happen over a period of months or even longer. How does one identify a bear market? Checking how an index is performing is one effective way of knowing whether the market is on a decline or not. For instance, S&P 500 and DJIA can be used to check for declining markets. When the S&P 500 has been lower than 15% for an entire past year, the market can be described as a bear market.

On the other hand, a bull market is the opposite of a bear market. In this case, a market can be described as a bull market when stock market prices experience a steady increase which is higher than the normal average. Just like in a bear market, indexes are used identify a bull market. For instance, if the average return on an index is usually 12% but for some reason it stays at 16% or above for some time, this is considered to be a bull market.

So, what causes a bull or bear market? It is worth mentioning that these markets fluctuate depending on the economic performance. If the economy is not performing well or there is a financial recession, the markets exhibit bearish characteristics and go down as a result of the bad economic times. If the economic times are bright and the market is doing well, the resultant effect is a bull market.

Some people see a bull market and get tempted to invest at that point. This is not a wise strategy because in some cases, some stock prices are usually at their peak and many people don't realize it. When you buy a lot of stocks when the prices have shot up, there is a risk of the price beginning to drop especially if you purchased them when they were at the peak price. Alternatively, the prices may fail to go up and therefore, you might not make any profits from the investment. The same concept applies for the bear market. You may decide to invest because stock prices are at the lowest and therefore, you expect them to begin increasing. However, there is a chance that they could keep going lower.

The ideal time to invest in the stock market is when the economy is performing well and out of recession. It is usually at this point when the markets begin to appreciate and it's difficult to predict what will happen in the near future. For investors looking to keep their risks low, it is important to ensure consistent investment and focus more on investing in a bull market and pay less attention to investing in a bear market because of the high uncertainty associated with it.

## What is Insider Trading?

Insider trading is a prohibited practice which refers to someone who buys or sells a security which they have access to the security's nonpublic information. It's important to note that insider trading is an unfair practice because when an insider is trading, they already have access to nonpublic information that other investors do not have. This gives an insider undue advantage because other investors don't have certain information about a security. Habits that constitute insider trading include passing sensitive information to certain individuals involved in the trade. Contrary to what people think, it is not only directors who can be held accountable for insider trading, brokers, family members or friends can also be guilty of this offence.

However, there are instances when insider trading becomes legal especially after material information regarding a security gets to the public domain and therefore nobody has undue advantage over the others. The SEC however requires that insiders should give an account of all their transactions. Since insiders have good knowledge about how their companies operate, it is good for investors to check and determine the legalities of every stock they wish to invest in.

A typical case of insider trading is where company owners, employees and other officers with information regarding a security purchase and sell stocks in their own companies or places of work. When partners engage in trading their own securities, they are required to furnish this information to the Securities and Exchange Commission. Insider trading is outlawed when one purchases or promotes a security while breaching the fiduciary responsibility.

Insider trading is a common habit that is practices in almost the financial markets across the globe. Accessing securities information that is not available to the rest of the public is regarded to be insider trading and doesn't really matter on which level this happens. The SEC prohibits this practice because it constitutes unfair trading and has a negative impact on the securities markets because it erodes the trust of investors.

It is however worth mentioning that insider trading is not easy to prove. The people who are involved in this practice are often professionals and therefore, know how to cover their dealings and escape detection. The punishment for insider trading is a jail term or fiscal penalty for convicted offenders. The SEC has also upgraded its penalties in a bid to curb those who participate in or entertain this illegal insider trading.

Utilizing nonpublic information for trading purposes is an offence that violates transparency which is a core principle of any financial market. In any transparent market, information and facts pertaining a security need to be displayed in a manner that allows all market participants to have access at the same time. This is critical because it is important to ensure that fair play prevails on financial markets and investors access the same information. Investors are only supposed to have an edge over the others based on the decisions they take after analyzing and interpreting the accessed data.

If a trader uses nonpublic information that is not accessible by the rest of the market to make financial gains, this is unfair and also compromises the quality of financial markets. If insider trading was to be permitted, investors would lose confidence in the entire system because they are aware some traders are enjoying benefits that others do not have.

### What are advances and declines?

The number of stocks that closes at a higher price than the previous day's close and the number of stocks that closes at a lower price than the previous day close is what is referred to as advances and declines. Experts look at advances and declines to analyze the general behavior of the stock market. Advances and declines form the basis of analytical tools like advance decline index, advance decline ratio and breath index.

Market indexes never tell traders the whole story about what happened in day trading. Another helpful piece of information that traders need to know is advances and declines. What market indexes only give you is a snapshot of representative stocks. Advances and declines numbers look at what each stock did and put them in three columns based on stock prices; declined, advanced and remained unchanged. The two important numbers are advanced or declines. These tell a trader how the market did overall and how the index stocks performed. This info gives a trader an idea of the status of the market. Advances and declines are calculated from the previous day close.

Advance and decline numbers are usually reported on radio and Television as advances led declines by a ratio of 2 to 1. This means that 2/3 of stocks are advanced and 1/3 is declined. Some may report advance and decline numbers as a ratio while other report them as percentage. To use advance and decline numbers, you need to understand the market first.

When it comes to using advances and declines, a trader must go with the numbers. In such a case, a trader must conclude the market was down despite what it was reported by the Dow. If there is any conflict between advances and decline numbers, go with the numbers and not the index to determine what the market really needs in terms of direction. As a trader, you need to know that a market that is important on one side of either advances or declines may have a challenge reversing out of that direction the following day. One of the major limitations of advances and declines is they don't inform a trader anything about the size of the advances/declines.

Another major way to use advances and declines is paying attention during the day to spot trends or false trends. Moreover, if a trader views a big movement in advances/declines numbers, it may be a signal of the change in indexes. Advances and declines number give you an indication of how the general market is doing and can add a level of information to indexes for a more clear understanding.

**What is the Bid price? What is the Ask price?**
In the trading world, we often come across the term bid price and ask price. What is the meaning of bid price and ask price? If you comprehend the two

prices, it will assist you to know more about the trade market. Actually, the bid price is the opposite to ask price or offer.

A two way price quotation which indicates the best price at which security can be sold and bought at a given time. The bid price represents the maximum price that a buyer is willing to pay for a security. The ask price is represents the minimum price that a seller is willing to receive for their security. A transaction occurs when a buyer and seller agrees on a price for the security.

The difference between the bid and asked price or spread is key indication of the liquidity of the asset. The smaller the spread, the better the liquidity also known as the bid and ask, bid offer and bid ask.

What is the bid price? A bid is the current highest price at which you could sell. In simpler terms, if you want to sell you gold, in generally, you can sell to the nearest to the bid price but not the bid price.

What is the Ask price? Ask is the opposite of bid. Ask is the current lowest price at which one can purchase. As a main rule, one can but it often higher than the ask price.

When you learn about these two terms, you need to know another term known as bid-ask spread. The difference between the bid price and ask price is known as the bid-ask spread. If you are keen on selling your gold, a broker will offer to purchase it for the bid price. On the other hand, if you like to purchase it, the broker will offer to buy it for the bid price. This is because no one likes to lose money in business.

For instance, the bid price $1420, the ask $1423. The spread for gold is (1423-1420=3). The broker than keeps the $3.00 traded. You need to keep in mind the most important of bid and ask price that buyer to pay and ask price and sellers once they receive the bid price.

The bid-ask spread is seen as a negotiation in progress. To be successful, traders need to be willing to take a stand and walk away in bid-ask spread through limit orders. By executing a market order without concern for the bid-ask and without insisting in a limit, traders can confirm another trader's bid and create a return for the trader.

Learning and understanding the bid-ask spread can help you in your investing strategy. As a trader, you need to know how to calculate the bid-ask spread and the basics of the bid-ask spread to gain more skills and knowledge.

**What is Short Selling?**

Short selling is a concept whereby you can sell a stock that doesn't belong to you with the aim of purchasing it back at a lower price and keep the difference. In most cases, this decision is taken when an investor suspects that the price of the stock is going to depreciate and not increase in value. Short selling is a key investment strategy which if used well can enable you to make good gains in the event that a market is going down. However, this technique is not for everyone but only those who understand it well and are willing to use it to increase their investment fortunes. Those who engage in this practice regularly find it very enticing and rewarding.

One question that is commonly asked by many people is 'how do you sell a stock that doesn't belong to you?' It's simple, your brokerage firm always make the stock available at short. In some cases, stocks are usually accessible to some brokers but not others. It is for this reason that investors interested in short selling usually prefer to open multiple accounts with numerous brokers. In order to do short selling, brokers have rules that trades are supposed to abide by. Broker accounts have to permit you participate in margin trading in order to qualify for short selling.

Of course, to participate in short selling, an investor needs to have funds readily available in order to purchase available stocks. It is important to note that you must have funds in your account in order to sell as stock. Just because you are selling a stock doesn't mean you shouldn't have money in your account. You need to have money to buy stocks on your account when you sell.

One major factor about short selling that sends cold shivers in investors is the possibility of getting losses. The fact that you are faced with the possibility of unlimited losses is something you have to think about carefully. It's also good to mention that your stockbroker is responsible for placing a margin call just in case the stocks depreciate to prevent you from losing your entire investment.

Why short selling? As mentioned earlier, a lot of investors do short selling in order to make cash on stock rises. This concept is usually useful when the overall stock market is low. Some investors go through long on a stock when it is appreciating and short when the stock begins to decrease in order to make profits from both sides.

If you are feeling nervous about investing your money in the stock market, one option good to learn about and consider using is short selling. This is because short selling strategies work well in both a bull and bear market. There are several sources of information where you can find more information about how to use short selling to make good profits in both a bear and bull market. Smart traders make an effort to learn other strategies that can improve their chances of making it in the stock market industry.

**What is a Dividend?**

The term dividend is commonly used in investment circles and refers to payments that a company remits to its shareholders usually on a quarterly basis. When a firm performs well in a given financial period, a portion of profits obtained are paid out to stockholders either as a dividend yield or cash distribution. When a firm obtains profits or gets a surplus at the end of a financial trading period, quarterly dividends are issued to shareholders. Companies that have realized profits can make use of their quarterly dividends in two ways; surplus can either be paid out as dividends or be re-ploughed back into the firm as retained earnings to fund key corporate development projects.

For the case of joint stock firms, quarterly dividends are issued at a fixed rate depending on the number of shares an investor has. This way, shareholders receive their dividends in direct proportion with the shares they own. It's worth mentioning that joint stock companies don't consider dividends as expenses but rather, they are considered as profits after tax and shared among shareholders.

Quarterly dividends

Quarterly dividends are issued out either as shares in the firm or cash distributions. In rare occasions, these dividends are issued as store credits. Retail consumer cooperatives are commonly associated with quarterly dividends based on their activity levels and scale of performance. Quarterly dividends are often considered a pretax expense and many firms opt to make these payments four times in a year. Using dividends, an investor can be able to buy extra company shares.

## Cash Distributions for shareholders

Dividend cash payments are paid in form of currency. Cash payments are usually submitted via electronic fund transfers and less commonly paper checks. Payments are known to be investment income and therefore, are subjected to taxation within the year payments are made. However, a lot of companies are using cash distribution as a technique of sharing company profits with shareholders. For every share you own, there is a specific dividend amount that is issue as a result of the shares you own. For instance, if you own 100 shares and the dividend per share amount is $1, your total dividend yield will be $100.

## Computing the Dividend Yield

A dividend yield is a method that shareholders use in order to determine how much cash they will earn for the shares they invested in a company. A dividend yield gives a hint of how much investors will receive after a firm makes profits. For this reason, it is important for investors to research widely and thoroughly in order to choose stable stocks that guarantee dividend payments. Larger and top performing companies are known for paying handsome dividends and therefore, their shares are always on high demand. In some cases, you can come across companies whose share value is high but they pay lower dividend yields. In such a case, you are better off choosing firms that are associated with high dividend yields because the cash distribution will be much higher.

## What is the P.E. ratio?

A lot of investors rely on the price of a stock to carry out analysis and determine where to invest. However, it is important to mention that price is not an accurate method of analyzing stocks and this is where PE ratio comes in. Using PE ratio for analysis is a wise idea because it means you are on the right track to choosing the best stocks and ultimately, having a good and rewarding investment portfolio. A lot of people will argue that price is an important factor in determining the stocks to choose which is true to some extent. However, when analysis for long term investment, knowing what PE ratio is and how it helps you to make good investment decisions is essential.

P/E is an abbreviation for Price/Earnings ratio. This ratio is the number that enables you to determine how much you are getting in return for your money. In simple terms, P/E ratio is the money investors are willing to part with for every $1 of earnings. For instance, if company A is currently trading at a P/E of 30, it means an investor is comfortable parting with $30 for $1 of the current earnings.

The best way to use this ratio is to compare it with other industry players within the same sector. For instance, if company A has a P/E of 52 and company B has a P/E of 15, the first thing that comes into mind is why would an investor want to commit their $52 for every dollar of their earnings for company A when they could only part with $15 per $1 for company B? This simply implies that firm A has a brighter future than company B and therefore, it will cost you more money to purchase shares with company A. In summary, company A is a better firm and has a balance sheet for those who want to see proof of performance. This is very important for any investor who is willing to make money using the stock market.

P/E ratio is only supposed to be used to compare firms in the same sector. You should therefore not use this ratio to make comparisons between firms in different sectors as it defeats logic and therefore, this ratio will not be useful to you in any way. For instance, you cannot compare the P/E ratio for a company in the hospitality industry with the P/E ratio of a company in the manufacturing sector. This is because these two companies deal with different products that are not related to each other in any way. The conditions of doing business and factors affecting business development are not the same.

Sometimes, you might find a company with great prospects but has a low P/E compared to other firms in the same category. If you come across such as scenario, feel free to purchase their stocks. On the other hand, you might come across a firm with a high P/E ratio but has a problematic balance sheet. It is for this reason that P/E ratio provides a comprehensive and all inclusive analysis for those who wish to invest.

**What is a Stock Split and a Reverse Stock Split?**
The main reason for people investing is to get income from dividends that are paid out by a company. Thanks to dividends, investors get a chance to either acquire more stocks or benefit from cash distributions whenever a company obtains profits. Firms usually opt to distribute dividends to its investors because of either not having enough funds to carry out major development projects or it simply wants to lower the price per stock to encourage more people to invest.

Reducing the price per stock increases share activity in the market and this is where a stock split becomes relevant. A stock split refers to an incredibly huge amount of dividend and its purpose is to increase the number of shares of a public company. In this case, the price per share undergoes adjustment so that the shares market capitalization doesn't change even after the split has been performed. As a result, the value of stock prices decreases paving way for increased liquidity.

It's worth mentioning that public companies always have a fixed number of shares that are put on the market. The decision to do a stock split is often decided by a firm's board of directors to increase the number of outstanding shares. For instance, for a 2-for-1 split, an investor who owns a single stock is given another extra share. In other words, if a firm has a total of 1 million shares in the market, a 2-for-1 split will make the shares rise to 2 million. In this case, the market capitalization remains constant but the share prices undergo the necessary adjustments. It's good to mention that a stock split can be in the ratio of 3-for-2, 3-for-1, 4-for-3, 5-for-2 and 5-for-4. In the case of fractional split, investors sometimes get their payments in cash instead of extra shares.

In the case of a 2-for-1 split, the price of a single share reduces to half its original value. Most companies decide to implement a stock split when they realize the share price is way too high compared to what other companies in the same market sector are offering their shareholders. The whole idea is to ensure that shares trade at affordable prices to raise liquidity and draw more investors.

One key advantage of a stock split is that it enables a firm to float more shares on the market. Thanks to stock split, smaller investors find the stock price friendly and therefore purchase more shares leading to increased demand. Furthermore, it could imply that the stock price has been continuously going up thus the need to decide on a stock split. When this happens, investors are assured they are investing in a good deal and this confidence in turn increases the value of shares.

There is also a reverse split which is the opposite of stock split. Here, shares not split but instead, they are combined in order to reduce the number of shares and increase the share price. In this case, the ratios are reversed. For instance, instead of 2-for-1, a reverse split is 1-for-2 with other ratios such as 1-for-3 and many others. However, on rare occasions do companies opt for reverse splits. Several institutional investors and mutual funds have implemented rules that discourage stock purchases of less than a certain amounts known to be minimum amounts. These restrictions are put because in the event the share prices fall too low, there is a risk of the stock being delisted from the exchange.

As an investor, knowing the difference between a stock split and reverse split and how it affects you is critical if you want to become a successful stock investor.

**What is Dollar Cost Averaging?**

If you have a savings plan that enables you to put your money in a certain amount of stocks or bonds every month, chances are high that your stock or bond price movements will give you good results if you practice dollar cost averaging. What is only required of you is to strictly follow your savings plan and place your money in an ideal investment venture such as bonds or stocks on a frequent basis.

What is dollar cost averaging? For instance if you are investing in a stock, dollar cost averaging will facilitate you to utilize your periodic savings amount to purchase more stocks when the share price is lower and pocket friendly. Furthermore, it will make you to purchase fewer shares when stock prices are more costly. The same concept applies whether you choose to invest in mutual funds, stocks, bonds or index funds.

Dollar cost averaging means that you come up with a specified amount of money to invest regularly and keep to the schedule regardless of any eventualities that take place in the stock market you are planning to invest. The same way you pay yourself first before repaying a debt of putting money in a savings account, dollar cost averaging advocates for the same.

It's worth mentioning that circumstances will come when you will make losses especially when stock prices depreciate. It's good to know that despite having dollar cost averaging, steady declines in stock prices will eventually lead to losses but if you adhere to your investment plan, chances are high that your investment will work in your favor in the long run. The only thing required of you is to be consistent with the amount of money you invest on a regular basis. You can also allow your savings remain on autopilot. A wise strategy is to set a fixed amount that can be deducted from every pay check that you get for the purpose of investment.

It is always good to monitor your dollar cost averaging investment and check your financial standing on a regular basis. It doesn't need to be too often, doing it annually is a good idea because regular checks can make you extremely nervous and cause you to abandon your plan and fail to realize your benefits. When you avoid making regular checks, you will not discover any complications with your savings strategy which might arise during the period of investment. A lot of financial advisors highly recommend that every investor should check on their dollar cost averaging investment and financial situation at least once in a year.

Succeeding as an investor requires a lot of sacrifice and discipline. Being consistent is the key to ensuring that you remain firmly on your investment path and realize your investment objectives. Dollar cost averaging has helped many investors to stay on course and understand the risks that are associated with different types of investment. Learning how to manage your finances and at the same time, keep investing requires careful balancing.

**What is a Margin Account?**

A margin account is an account that is offered by brokerages that gives an investor the opportunity to borrow money to purchase securities. An investor can put 50% of the value of a purchase and borrow the remaining from a broker. A broker charges an investor interest for the right to borrow money and uses securities as collateral. Calculation on how to margin works can be a bit complicated but one can learn about.

One of the essential things to understand about margin is that it comes with consequences. Margin is leverage which in simple terms means, your gains and losses are amplified. Having a margin account is a great when your investments are increasing in value. It's not advisable for a beginner to venture in margin exposes an investor to a lot of risks. Margin is a great tool for experienced or advanced investors, so until you have learnt the game, play it safe.

Investing on margin is not the same with gambling, but it can draw some parallels between margin trading and casino. Having a margin account is a high-risk strategy that can yield a lot of profit if executed the right way. On the other hand, the negative side of margin is that an investor can lose their all their investments. One of the things riskier that investing on margin is investing on margin without understanding what you are doing.

Once an investor gets a margin account, they start margin trading. Purchasing on margin can also be viewed asking for a loan from your brokerage. Margin trading gives an investor the opportunity to purchase more stocks than they would be able to normally. To trade on margin, one needs a margin account. A margin account is very different from regular cash account and one can use it to trade using the money in the account. By law, a broker is required to obtain a signature to open a margin account. The margin account can be part of an investor's standard account opening agreement or a different agreement. An initial investment of at least $2000 is needed for a margin account (some brokerages may ask for more). Once the account is opened and is operational, an investor can go ahead and borrow up to 50% of the purchase price of a stock.

An investor can keep their loan as long as they want as long as they fulfill their obligations. After an investor sells their stock in a margin account, the proceeds go to their broker against the repayment of the loan until it is fully paid. Borrowing money definitely comes with a cost and in this case, margin securities act as the collateral. This also means that an investor will need to pay the interest on their loan. Therefore, purchasing on margin is commonly used for short-term investments. The longer an investor holds an investment, the greater the return that is required to break even. If an investor holds an investment on margin for a long period, chances are high that they will make a profit stacked against them.

# Chapter Seven
## Swing Trading

## What is Swing Trading?

There are a lot of similarities between swing trading and day trading. Swing trading refers to a technique that traders use to reap good profits from a quick buy and sell cycle. The key thing to note about swing trading is that it takes traders a longer time to realize good profits as compared to day trading where everything is completed within some seconds, minutes or hours. The traditional timings for swing trading are known either days or weeks.

Some tactics for day trading cannot apply to swing trading. It is challenging to get the difference between the bid and ask price in order to obtain a profit. The swing trader is more focused on the stock price trends over allocated time periods. In order to realize profits in swing trading, you must have good market knowledge and know what is available. To some extent, you should be able to make some basic market predictions especially in the near future. If the market continues to exhibit bullish behavior, a buy and hold strategy in this case outperforms swing trading. If a swing trader is purchasing stocks and disposing them off after a few days later, the chances of missing out on price gains in between the time stocks are sold and the next ones purchased is high. However, in a bear market, nobody does well and the swing trader is also affected.

The best condition for swing trading is in times when the market is showing stability over time. When the index remains at the same place or gradually increases, the swing trader has the perfect chance to come into the market and chase their goals without having to be there for a long time. Traders always have a challenging task trying to determine what the future holds for stock markets which makes swing trading a risky affair.

Swing trading is excellent opportunity for traders to become more knowledgeable with the market. Swing trading can still give traders good profits especially if you perfect your trading skills and plan on moving to day trading in the coming days. For beginners, day trading is not advisable because it involves a lot of technicalities and traders are required to comply with specified minimums in order to avoid account freezing because of low equity to cater for margins.

For many investors, the buy and hold strategy is not an easy task compared to swing trading which is considered more exciting and friendlier. Thanks to swing trading, you can dispose your stocks within a few days or weeks and begin to see profits streaming in. swing trading is an excellent way to keep traders motivated and encourage them to expand their investments in the stock market. So, if you are planning to venture into stock trading, it is good to first begin trading as a swing trader until you are comfortable and skilled enough to switch to day trading. Swing trading has served as the starting point for many successful stock traders.

**How to Get Started Swing Trading**

Swing trading has been identified as a good technique especially for traders who are still new and want to trade in a comfortable environment that allows them to learn. Every trade is in the market with the sole aim of making profits and therefore, it is up to you to choose whether you prefer swing trading or day trading. A lot of investors love swing trading because it offers a higher chance of making good profits without having to be around fulltime and tied to your desk to monitor stock movements. Thanks to the ability to put stops and targets, you can comfortably swing trade despite being committed to a fulltime career.

Day traders rely on stock changes within very short periods of time to make profits and can participate in several trades in a single day. On the other hand swing traders enjoy comfort and stress free trading because they can wait for several days before initiating a transaction. Because of the fewer transactions, the stress and hassle for swing traders is less.

What makes swing traders to trade? Whenever there are any changes either upwards or downwards, these traders are forced to trade. In an uptrend, there is a recurring series of both higher highs and higher lows indicating that the stock is receiving enough market support to trade at higher prices. When the price begins to drop, it doesn't go as far as it did during previous declines. For a downward trend, the scenario is the opposite.

When a genuine upward trend is visible, swing traders begin figure out how to enter the market. The most ideal time to purchase the stock is when the price takes a slight drop while on an uptrend. Swing traders rely on stops to reduce losses and safeguard their gains.

A swing trading setup is useful especially when you want to get started with swing trading. It's important to mention that stock trade in cycles. It is normal for stocks to go up and down because they never move towards a single direction forever. Usually, in most cases after several consecutive days of moving in one direction, prices always take an immediate reversal. The good news is that swing trading works well with almost any stock however, it's known to perform extremely well with indexes. Some of the recommended trading platforms are S&P500, Down, NASDAQ. There are different types of swing trading tutorials that you can use to prepare yourself for trading. Some tutorials have complicated setups but there are some which are simpler and interesting to learn.

A typical set-up:

- Identify a stock whose prices have been appreciating consecutively for at least 7 days
- At the close of the 7th day, sell short
- Buy back at the previous low

With a simple strategy illustrated above, you should be able to realize good profits and earn thousands of dollars every week. You just need to make sure that you practice good money management habits in order to achieve your goals.

**What Is The Difference Between Swing Trading and Day Trading?**
Day trading and swing trading are two common terms that you are likely to come across in trading. As an active trader, day trading and swing trading are very similar. Both these trade methodologies are keen on short-term profits based on price fluctuations in the market. In this article, we are going to discuss the key difference between swing trading and day trading.

One of the major differences between day trading and swing trading is level of effort required. Day trading requires an investor to analyze the market and every day and make fast decisions. One is more likely to trade during specific time frames; morning and afternoon. On the other hand, swing trade allows someone to catch their breath. One can be able to watch their stocks to make sure they are not breached.

Day trading and swing trading also defer in trade profit exceptions. Day trading requires one to make more money per trade if they want to be successful on the long run. This means that the profits range from 5% up to few percentages. Another thing worth mention is that day trading needs one to have a target in mind.  Swing trading provides a more large profit potential than day trading. In a normal day, you can shoot a few percentages points all the way up to 20% and beyond.  Since the timeframe is for trading is bigger, the profit targets are also bigger.

Swing trading does not need you to place trades daily. The trades take place every two to three weeks. The time is more because one needs to provide the stock ability to swing from one price to another. On the other hand, day trading means opening and closing trades within the same day. It is possible to trade once per day up to hundred trades.

Another difference between swing trading and day trading is money management. Day trading allows one to use up to four times of their available money to purchase and sell securities.  One is required to make fast decisions on how much they will allocate per trade. This also requires one to track how much of their money is in float and having an understanding the margin requirements of their brokerage firm.  When it comes to swing trading, it allows one to trade with a maximum of two times of their available money.

Day trading is more risky but provides more control over your trading activity. At this point, it's possible to feel how hard the stock is trending and can quickly make thing go haywire. On the other hand, swing trading is less risky because of the less margin used per trade.  Another difference between day and swing trading is the instant gratification.  In day trading, one can measure their performance on a daily basis and know when they winner or not.  As for swing trading, one requires to have more patience from a few days or up to eight weeks.  This waiting period always depends on how well the stock trends.

Another main difference between day and swing trading is the startup capital required. In day trading, you need a starting capital of 50 to 1, cash to take care of start your day trader. As for swing trading, you can hold onto your full time job because the amount required to start up trading depends on your own financial capabilities. If you are planning on swing trading long term, you need 100 to 1 cash to expenses. The reason why this amount is higher compared to day trading is because you may be in trade for a longer period and you become unable to use trading profits to pay off your living expenses.

In conclusion, when it comes to the differences between day trading and swing trading, you can understand them better by figuring whether you are trading for a living? How much money you have to trade? What's your appetite risk? Or are risk taker?  By answering some these questions truthfully, you will be able to know which type of trading best suits you.  You need to take enough time to understand day trading and swing trading properly to be able to choose one that will bring you profits.

**What Is Considered A Good Swing Trading Return?**

Are you interested to be a swing trader? It's a great idea because a lot of people are already swing trading. Actually, many new traders try their luck at the market casino each year. Unfortunately, most end up losing more money and the bright side a lot wiser. Things can turn out better for you and you can get it right from the start.

As a new trader, you need to equip yourself with helpful swing trading tips that will shorten your learning duration and get you on the right path to make profits. Good advice goes much further when it comes to trading longevity.

If your goal is to trade for a living and you want to have money in your account soon. You must be willing to wait and keep watching the markets, paper trade and gain experience needed by any beginner. Pre trading preparation requires a certain degree of risk in the process. Paper trading lets you consider all the angles without losing any money. However, you need to know you can realize what it's possible to draw down and end up losing money with real trades.

The challenge is there is a lot to learn from swing trading that you won't understand until you get in to the trading system. This means that you have no any other choice but to start trading and learn the hard way. Actually, the nature risk that you choose determines the overall success or failure in the markets.

One of the main questions that most traders ask is what is the good swing trading return? What percentage is my portfolio should put to work on any trade? Traders are usually different from each other and approach the market in different ways. Some traders do this part time and risk a small percentage of capital. On the other hand, some do this full time and place a high percentage of equity t risk in each trade.

When it comes to swing trading, it's not as hard as science rocket. It's a way to get an edge to profit from trades. Each swing trader chooses to enter and leave the market in a different way. The average returns are all over the map for those who double their money every six months to those who can't meet the interest rates in their checking accounts.

If you are wondering if it's realistic as a new trader to grow your account by 5% to 10% a month, you need to know that returns of 5% to 10% a month are completely unrealistic especially for a new trader. As a new trader, you should focus on the dynamics that generate price movement and not worry about making money. New traders need to pay attention on the dynamics that generate price movement and worry less about making money. These processes take a long time to comprehend. Trying to make money interferes with trading education because it creates various types of performance anxiety issues. What is important is to learn and understand how to swing trade well and the money will eventually follow.

# Chapter Eight
## Day Trading

## What is Day Trading?

Day traders differ from investors in that day traders hold their securities for a day. They close out of their positions at the end of the day and start all over again the following day. As for swing traders, they hold securities for days or even months and investors can hold for years.  The short-term nature of day trading reduces a lot of risks because there no chances of something happening overnight to cause losses. Some investors usually retire for the day thinking their position is in perfect shape only to wake up with the news that the company has announced terrible earnings or fraud charges.

On the flip side, day trader's choices of positions and securities has to work out in a day, there is no tomorrow for any position. Swing traders or investors have the privilege of adequate time and they take some time for a position to work out. When it comes to trading, markets are important and prices reflect all information about a security.  When you decide to take up day trading, the rules that may have assisted you pick stocks or find awesome mutual funds over the years may no longer apply.

Day trading is a hectic business. Traders work in front of their computer, reacting to blips that represent real money. Traders are expected to make quick decisions because their ability to make money depending on the successfully executing of large number of trades that generate small profits. This because they close out their positions in the futures, options and stocks contracts they own at the end of the day but risks are limited.

Those limits on risk can get in the way for profits. Furthermore, a lot can happen in a year thus increasing the likelihood that your trade idea will work out. In a day, you need to be patient and work fast. You need to know that there are some days there is nothing to buy.

Day trading has different styles of days trading that are suited for different day trader's personalities. These styles range from short term trading such as scalping where positions are held for a few minutes to longer-term swing position trading where positions are held throughout trading day. Most day trading systems have a lot of flexibility and have vacant positions for anywhere and from a few minutes or hours depending on how the trade is going.  Some traders may trade in multiple styles but most of them choose a single style and take only one type of trade.

Day trading also has various types of trade which include trend trades, ranging trades and counter trend trades. Trend trades are trades in the direction of the current price movement and counter trend trades are trades against the direction of the current price movement. Ranging trades are traders go back and forth between two process and are used when the market in moving sideways.  A lot of day traders will choose a single type of trade but some traders choose other different types depending on the current condition of the market.

When it comes to style and type of day trading, there are other different day traders. Some day traders also like to make trades throughout the trading day while others prefer to wait for what they consider as the best time for them to start trading.

**How Much Money Do I Need To Start Day Trading?**

How much money do I need to start day trading? Is one of the most asked questions by people who want to start day trading stocks. How much money you need depends on the styles of trading you want to do, where you trade and the instruments that you trade.

Day trading stocks in US requires an investor to maintain an account balance of $25, 000. An investor need to start with at least $30,000 or more if they plan to make more than four-day trades per trading week. If their account drops below $25,000, they won't be in a position to continue day trading until they add their account to more than $25,000.

It is possible to day trade on other global markets without this minimum balance. As a trader, you can open a day trading account of at least $10,000 if you are short term trading outside US. With smaller accounts than this, fees can be a large challenge to overcome. Another thing to note is stocks are traded in 100 share lots, therefore, a small amount of capital limits the stocks which can be traded.

Even with these minimums are in a position to enter the market, it's important to remember that one of the main mistake traders make before starting to trade begins undercapitalized. As investor needs to keep in mind that losses take place and they need to account for this fact. When one goes through losses, they need to have adequate money to keep trading.

Experts recommend traders to only taking a risk of at most 1% of their capital on trade. Their risk is defined a difference in price between their entry price and their stop loss level plus multiplied by the number of shares they have. The minimum equity requirement for a trader who is a pattern day trader is $25,000. This amount ($25,000) requirement must be deposited into the traders account before any day trading activities and must be maintained at all times. A trader needs to know that each day trading account is required to meet this amount ($25,000) independently by using the financial resources available in the account.

As an investor, you also need to understand day trading buying power. A trader who sees himself as patter day trader can trade up to four times their customer's maintenance excess within the close of the previous day equity securities. If a trader exceeds the day trading purchasing power limitation, the broker dealer issues a day trading margin call. The trader is given five business days to meet his maintenance margin excess based on their daily total trading commitment for equity securities. If a trader doesn't meet the margin call after the five businesses, the day trading account is restricted to trading only on cash available for 90 days until the call is achieved.

When it comes to how much money you need to start day trading, one thing every trader, investor or customer needs to know is how to make profits from day trading.

**How To Start Day Trading?**
Venturing in day trading can seem like a daunting task because there is a lot of information that you need to know before you start day trading. Once you have a good understanding of the basics, you can start trading with confidence. Nowadays, there are a lot of tutorials and articles that provide all the information that you need to commence day trading and assist you with various tasks such as choosing a day trading brokerage, charting software, setting up your trading, managing your first trade and picking a market.

If you have started day trading or you are planning of becoming a day trader, these sources will provide enough information you need to get started. Topics and articles such as introduction to day trading, day trading markets and tools needed in day trading provide a good understanding of the basics. With this foundation, you can be able to proceed on day trading with confidence.

When it comes to choosing a day trading brokerage firm, you need to know that these day trading brokerages are different from traditional investment brokerages because they offer services designed for day trading. These reviews and profiles of day trading brokerages explain the criteria that an investor needs to look at when choosing a day trading brokerage including market data feeds, accessibility, available markets, trading software features, commissions and fees.

There are different day trading markets with their own character and each is suited with a different style of trading. The discussion of best markets for beginning day traders will help you to choose the markets that are right for you by covering helpful topics such as maintenance margin requirements, volatility and initial among others. Once you have chosen your markets, the market profiles provide the market's trading information such as market holidays and contract specifications.

With the advance in technology, day trading tools has also changed. Modern trading is electronic and the exchanges are handled by computers which are made available over the internet. This means that traders can work from anywhere in the world by using tools and services. Some of these tools used in day trading include internet, telephone and computer. Other tools are services used specifically for trading such as real time market data and direct access brokerage.

These tools are hardware, software and other physical items that are needed for day trading. Each item is explained in detail with an explanation of when and how the item is used in day trading. The tools are the services that are needed to progress in day trading. Each service is described in detail with an explanation of when and how the service is used during trading.

All in all, day trading is not rocket science because it can be easily learnt. All you have to do is to take enough time to learn and understand the key point required to successfully day trade. With enough experience and knowledge, you will be able to make profits in day trading.

## Chapter Nine
## Stock Instruments Traded

**What are the Instruments Traded in the Stock Market?**

With the high number of people looking for affordable and safe investment options, the stock market has provided a safe haven for people looking to save and better their financial future. Before investing in the stock market, it is good to understand what you are getting into in order to make the right decisions that will safeguard your investment. Before investing in the stock market, it is wise to ensure that you get adequate professional advice in order to determine the right investment for you. The stock market is a vast industry with many types of investment and understanding each investment and evaluating its suitability for meeting your investment objectives is critical.

In case you want to be part of the stock market, they are different types of instruments that you can use to attain your financial objectives. Some of the common investment types are stocks, mutual funds, IPO's, Futures and Options. The first step of becoming a successful investor is to understand the definition of each investment instrument, its characteristics and how it can be beneficial to you. Below are definitions of common investment instruments used in the stock market.

Shares: A share is a stock that is sold to investors by a company and represents a unit of ownership. When an investor buys shares in a company, they buy a piece of the company. It is however important to understand that shares are distributed amongst many investors and therefore, ownership is represented in terms of a very small percentage. When you are a shareholder in a company, you have voting rights but lack the power to make key decisions affecting a company.

Mutual Funds: Unlike shares which are owned by individuals, mutual funds bring together a group of investors. Here, a portfolio manager is appointed and tasked with the responsibility that money collected from investors is invested in a suitable investment opportunity that will guarantee good returns.

IPO: IPO is an abbreviation of Initial Public Offer and refers to a scenario where a company advertises its stocks for the first time to the general public. Companies use IPOs to raise money for funding various corporate development projects. An IPO presents a good opportunity for an investor to enter the stock market with the hopes of making good returns.

Futures: This is a financial contract that obligates a either a buyer to acquire an asset or a seller to dispose an asset which includes a stock at a date and price which are already predetermined. Futures contracts include the both the quality and quantity of the asset in question and they are standardized to enable trading on a futures exchange. The futures market is characterized by its capability to make use of a high leverage relative to the stock market.

Options: This is a contract that allows a buyer the freedom to buy or sell an asset for an agreed price on or before the specified date. An option works the same way as a bond or stock because it also acts as a security. It's worth mentioning that this contract is binding and comes with a set of defined terms.

**Stocks Vs Mutual Funds**

Before investing, it is important to have a good idea about the type of investment you're willing to pursue. Nowadays, there are several investment options to choose from. Depending on your budget, objectives and preference, you can choose between Stocks and Mutual Funds. However, a lot of investors especially beginners fail to differentiate between Mutual Funds and Stocks. Knowing where to invest your money between the two in order to get the best returns can be a challenge.

Both stocks and mutual funds have their own advantages and disadvantages and therefore, it is hard to determine which of the two investment options is ideal. So, how do you determine the best investment choice? The personal circumstances under which you intend to invest is the best strategy to use to choose between stocks and mutual funds. To be in a better position to understand which option will work for you best, you need to know the difference between the two.

Stocks refer to company shares which investors can either sell or buy using the stock market. Stocks are known to be a good investment channel but are high risk and therefore, investors should be well informed before venturing into stocks. Furthermore, stock market prices are always affected by prevailing market circumstances. On the other hand, the process of investing in mutual funds is somewhat different. In this case, fund managers are responsible for collecting money from several investors and channeling the collected money into various investment ventures such as bonds, stocks or other assets. It is the role of the fund manager to use their expertise to research and find the best form of investment.

In the case of stocks, once you purchase stocks, you automatically become a shareholder in the company you have invested in. For mutual funds, you hand over your money to a fund manager who uses their expertise and market knowledge to choose an investment they think will grow faster and bring the highest returns.

The 3 main factors that can be used to determine whether you should choose to invest in mutual funds or stocks are; Expenses, Returns and Risks.

Risks: If you are concerned about risks jeopardizing your investment, going for mutual funds is a wise decision. This is because mutual funds allow you to diversify your investment by putting your money in different projects and assets. Mutual funds are considered an excellent choice for beginners because good performing investments cover up for underperforming projects. Stocks are considered to be extremely risk because they limit you to investing in a single company especially if you're on a tight budget and cannot diversify.

Returns: Stocks that suffer from fewer risks have a better potential of generating good income than mutual funds. When fund managers invest collective investor money in some projects, profit margins are substantially lowered making it challenging to achieve good returns. In the case of stocks, investing in the right company and at the right time yields good profits.

Expenses: When it comes to investment expenses, stocks are the preferred option because they are cheaper to maintain. Mutual funds are associated with costs such as Implicit, Explicit and hidden costs.

Based on the above factors and understanding the difference between the two, you should be in a position to make a wise choice.

### Common Stocks vs Preferred Stocks

In case you are planning to invest in the stock market, there are two major types of stocks; common stocks and preferred stocks. However, to make the best decisions, it is important to understand the difference between the two in terms of issuance, financial terms and rights to ownership. It is important for you as an investor to research well before making any decisions. You shouldn't believe that preferred stocks are better than common stocks just because of their titles. Each type of stock has its own characteristics, advantages as well as disadvantages. Understanding the key differences between the two types of stocks is the best way to make a wise choice.

Common stocks

Common stocks are popular among every investor and purchasing them represents owning a piece of the company you have invested in. Here, stocks owners receive dividends whenever a company realizes profits usually computed on a quarterly basis. As a firm expands, there is an increase in dividends which in turn motivates investors to pay higher for a stock. Aside from receiving dividends, investors also benefit from appreciation of a stock value. Traditionally, 40% value of a stocks return is dividend while the rest 60% is obtained from value appreciation.

Owners of common stocks have the right to vote and participate in elections to put in place the firm's board of directors. In the event of bankruptcy, shareholders are only paid after creditors, bond holders and preferred stock owners have received their payments. Because of this, some people find a common stock a risky investment compared to preferred stocks. On the brighter side, common stocks come with more handsome returns.

Preferred Stock

These stocks also represent ownership in a company. Preferred stocks are classified as securities sharing characteristics of both bonds and stocks. Similar to a bond, a preferred stock comes with a fixed dividend that owners are entitled to receive annually. Preferred stock owners are not allowed to vote and decide how a company will be managed.

Preferred stocks come with a fixed dividend despite the fact that preferred share values often fluctuate. It's worth mentioning that preferred stocks come with no maturity date like bonds. If a firm doesn't pay a dividend, this doesn't mean a firm is bankrupt. On the other hand, failure to repay a bond is an indication of bankruptcy. In this case, a company has the option to skip dividend payments for its preferred shareholders but all unpaid dividend amounts must be paid before common stock dividends are paid out. Because preferred stock shareholders earn their dividends before common stock shareholders, this is the reason why they are called preferred stocks.

In summary, common stocks are common amongst shareholders and can be purchased to diversify investment. You can purchase common stocks to add onto your investment portfolio of preferred shares or bonds. For those interested in long term financial planning, preferred stocks are a wise idea. However, to be on the safe side, make sure you talk to your financial advisor and understand the differences between the two types of stocks.

**What is a Stock Option?**

Stock option trading helps investors to boost their leverage and achieve higher rates of return as compared to simple stock trading. For instance, an investor can select stocks that appreciate in value within a short period of time with a possibility of realizing an increase of 10 to 15 times. It's worth mentioning that the investor has to determine the period within which the increase will occur. In the recent times, the concept of stock option trading has become popular among investors despite the real risks that stock option trading comes with. However, despite the risks, there are three main reasons that still attract investors to this type of trading. These are; Speculation, Employee Stock Option and Hedging.

Employee Stock Options: A lot of companies decide to use stock options to retain talented employees at their premises. For the case of employees, they are an option but are not obliged to buy company shares. This is done with the hope that share prices will increase and then enable the option holder to purchase stocks at the option price. The shareholder can then sell shares immediately and make profits or keep them with the hope that prices will continue to rise and therefore, create an opportunity for more profits.

Speculation: Since they present several options for an investor, it is possible for you to make profits when the market goes up and remains the same. This is a special feature that traditional shares lack. With speculation, you have to try and predict the movement of a stock i.e. whether it will go up, down or remain at the same level. When the prices go up, it presents an opportunity for you to make a lot of money however you can also lose substantially when prices are on a declining trend.

When you speculate, you need to be in a position to not only predict stock movement directions but also know the magnitude of movements as well as the timeframe within which all these movements will take place. Speculation is beneficial when dealing with stock option because this way, investors can use leverage to their advantage. For instance with one options contract, you can be in charge of 50, 100, 200 or a higher number of shares. If you are in charge of a huge number of shares, you don't require significant movement in the prices of shares to obtain good profits.

Hedging: Investors benefit from stock option trading thanks to hedging which has similarities with insurance. We always insure cars, homes, rental properties and our health against unexpected eventualities. In the same case, options come in handy to have your investments insured against stock downturns. Despite the fact that hedging benefits large companies, individuals also stand to benefit. For instance, if you are interested to trade in stocks with hopes of getting profits from better prices but at the same time, you need to limit your losses, hedging your investment is a good idea. By doing this, you can be able to make good profits when the price appreciates. If prices dip, you losses are still limited because of the 'insurance' you took using the options contract.

**What is a Mutual Fund?**

Mutual funds have been defined differently in various investment platforms and it is easy for a layman to easily get confused. However, the simplest definition of a mutual fund is that it is an investment plan which is collectively managed where funds are obtained from a wide variety of investors. The funds obtained are then put into various investment ventures such as stocks, bonds and various types of assets. In mutual funds, each investor has shares which constitute part of the portfolio.

As mentioned earlier, mutual funds are invested in different types of securities such as bonds, cash instruments and stocks with various sub categories. Funds that are invested in stocks can put into a specific industry such as energy, technology or utilities and are referred to as sector funds. It's worth mentioning that mutual funds are always managed and supervised by a professional manager whose role is to evaluate performance of the investment by forecasting, checking cash flowing in and out by investors amongst other critical roles. A portfolio manager is also responsible for selecting investments and monitoring them to ensure that investment objectives are achieved.

How to make money from mutual funds

You can get a return on investment through stocks or interest obtained on bonds. The fund issues distributions to fund holders which is income that is obtained throughout the year. When the fund disposes of a security that holds a lot of value, it makes a capital gain and the profit is distributed amongst investors. In case the fund holdings appreciate in the price and the manager doesn't sell them, the value of the shares of the fund increases. Also, you can be able to sell your individual shares for purposes of making profits. The fund also allows you the freedom to use your received distribution check either to increase your shares or reinvest your money.

Mutual Funds Advantages

There are reasons why many investors opt to select mutual funds as their investment vehicles. To begin with, these funds are professionally managed and therefore, you have the guarantee that a qualified professional will take care of your investment. This is important especially if you don't have the time or qualifications to watch over your stocks. For small investors, mutual funds are an excellent way to engage the services of a full-time manager to look after their money and make wise investment decisions.

When you invest in mutual funds, you have the chance to diversify your investment to a wide variety of industry sectors. This is something that is usually impossible for a small investor to manage. The risk is well spread out which is good because there are less chances of encountering risks that will jeopardize your investment.

Economies of scale: Transaction costs associated with mutual funds are much less because mutual funds transact securities involving a huge amount of money.

Just like individual stocks, mutual funds are very convenient because they can be easily converted into cash at any time.

Investing in a mutual fund is simple because for as low as $ 100, it is possible to put your money in a mutual fund and expect to see some good returns.

**What is a Mutual Fund's N.A.V?**

NAV otherwise known as Net Asset Value is a representation of the share market value of a fund. NAV refers to the price investors pay (bid price) to acquire fund shares from a company and dispose them of (redemption price) to give money to a company. NAV is calculated by taking into account the sum value of all securities and cash in a fund's portfolio and subtracting any liabilities, by the amount of outstanding shares. NAV calculations are done at the end of the day derived from trading days after closing market prices of securities have been factored into consideration.

For instance, a fund with an asset base of 50 million and liabilities of 10 million, the net asset would be 40 million. NAV is an important value for investors because it sheds light on share trading. From NAV is always used to calculate a fund's price per unit. When you divide a fund's NAV by the number of outstanding units, the resulting figure will be the price per unit.

Mutual Funds NAV is therefore simply defined as a fund's Net Asset Value. Shares here are traded daily characterized by different daily share trading prices. It's important to mention that every mutual fund has a Net Asset Value per share that is calculated on a daily basis based on the closing market prices for that day and shares of other securities included in the investment portfolio.

The daily NAV is based on every buy or sell order as well as shares for mutual funds. The investor doesn't know the trade price of the transaction that took place until the following day. It's worth mentioning that mutual funds release all their income and capital gains to the fund holders. Monitoring NAV changes is the best way to determine performance. However, a comprehensive analysis can also be obtained by measuring the annual total return.

It's worth mentioning that ETF and closed end mutual trade similarly as stocks on the financial markets. Because of this, shares involved in this trade do so at market value which can either be below which implies trading at a discount or above (trading at a premium) the actual NAV of the fund undergoing trade.

Just like stock are traded on markets daily, Exchange Traded Funds (ETFs) undergo the same process with their value per share commonly referred to as Net Asset Value per share or NAV. In summary, this is the value per share of a given mutual fund which is obtained by dividing the sum value of all securities contained in a fund's portfolio subtracted from any liabilities by total number of shares outstanding at the period of calculation. Net Asset Value per share is a key value that mutual fund investors need to understand how it is calculated and interpret it correctly for their benefit.

The most critical thing to know is that Mutual Fund NAVs undergo daily changes and therefore, you cannot rely on them fully to get a good idea of how your portfolio is performing. It's worth mentioning that factors such as distribution affect mutual fund's NAV making it difficult to track performance.

## What is a 401(k) Plan?

The real reason for being employed or having an income is not just to live a comfortable life now but rather, setting aside finances to plan and safe for a comfortable and rewarding future. Your success in the future all depends on how much effort you put into saving now especially the mode of your investment. Once you a job, there are several investment opportunities that will come your way and it is important to make wise decisions because your decisions will determine what kind of retirement you will have.

In simple terms, 401k plan assists you to put aside some savings in order to guarantee a quality life after retirement. If you like, you can call it a revised form of pension plans. In order to make the right choices, you need to educate yourself about the available plans. Some of the firms include the 401k plan in the package in order for their customers to have a better understanding of the retirement plan.  In most cases, firms withhold a portion of an employee's income and keep it aside in a savings account. This is a typical 401k plan and is the most common and basic form.

Another technique of having a 401k plan is to open an investment account. By doing this, you can be able to save money and be in more control of your savings than the traditional 401k approach. The stock market is commonly associated with this arrangement with the investor expected to fully understand the level of risks involved.

The main reason for having a 401k plan is to ensure employees have a bright and happy retirement. Unlike mutual funds, stock market or bonds, 401k plan is left to your discretion since matters relating to retirement are personal and highly depend on the decisions you take. Knowing that 401k revolves around your retirement, it is good to make good decisions that will benefit you in the future.

If you are willing to be part of the 401k plan, it means that you will give consent to allow a specified percentage of your monthly salary to be put into a savings account. The money that is put aside is put into mutual funds and other investment ventures in order to grow your money. The good thing is that your these plans allow your contributions to grow without being taxed. You are only taxed if you decide to withdraw cash from a 401k account.

When withdrawing from a 401k account, you need to think about the costs. The good news is that as a member, you are allowed to borrow a loan from 401k and pay back with an interest. Alternatively, you can withdraw your funds and opt not to return to the plan. However, remember that there are taxes that you need to pay. For people under the age of 60, the taxes are even higher.

Consider yourself lucky if your firm matches a specific percentage of the amount you give out because this will spearhead faster accumulation and growth of your funds. The advantage of 401k plans is that you can move with them even after changing jobs.

Apart from getting your contribution, the money is not just left idle, it is invested in stocks, bonds or mutual funds. This is an effective arrangement for those intending to save towards a comfortable retirement. 401k plan discourages investors from removing money from the program because you are supposed to saving for your old age. Therefore, to discourage frequent withdrawals, those wishing to withdraw have to pay high taxes and penalty fees.

**What is an IPO?**

What is one thing that large public companies share in common? Aside from being well established and having a widely known reputation in their area of expertise, they all went through an IPO or initial public offering. IPO stands for Initial Public Offering and is a terminology that any investor interested in the stock markets must have come across. An IPO is widely used in the financial and investment circles to refer to a period where a company for the very first time advertises its shares to the general public in order to attract investors. Using an IPO, a firm's shares can be freely transacted in the stock market through both buying and selling.

It is important to mention that shares advertised to the general public are only a portion of the firm and not 100% representation of a company. It is only a specified percentage of a firm's shares that are allocated to the public using an IPO. In most cases, company owners or the board of directors usually retain a large percentage of the shares. In order to understand better what an IPO is, it is good to determine the objectives of an IPO.

So, why does a company offer an IPO?
The main reason why companies opt for an IPO is because it is an excellent strategy to raise funds for a company. A lot of firms plan to utilize the funds obtained from an IPO to carry out key business development projects such as expansion in order to achieve growth and ultimately, improve financial performance. Most companies know that an IPO is an excellent way to raise funds from the public but there are also disadvantages of an IPO. The downside of initial public offers is that companies planning for an IPO are forced to comply with strict legal and financial regulations in order to be cleared by the authorities.

So, what happens in an IPO Process?
The initial step for any firm intending to offer an IPO is to liaise with a couple of investment banks to act as underwriters. Underwriters play an important role because their work is to carry a comprehensive assessment and evaluation of a business by closely examining the financial background and operational capacity in order to determine how many shares of a company need to be sold out to the public. Once an agreement has been reached, a company enters into an agreement with the lead underwriter giving them the authority to begin selling the shares to interested investors.

In the case of large organizations dealing with shares running into billions, many huge investment banks may be required to play the role of underwriters. These banks always earn commissions for every share that they sell to the general bank and it's therefore okay to call them agents. Underwriters also assist a company selling its shares comply with any legal and financial requirements.

A lot of multinationals firms that plan on holding an IPO in a specific country are required to ensure full compliance with the rules that govern that specific country they intend to have an IPO. In some instances, law firms are called upon to interpret the law and assist clients to achieve full compliance with the local systems.

Immediately an IPO is launched, firms are required to hand over their yearly business earnings reports to the financial securities board now that the company's shares will be officially listed on the stock market.

As an investor, it is good to understand what an IPO is and how it can improve your chances of building a solid investment portfolio that will give you good financial returns.

## Chapter Ten
## Reports and Analysis

**What is Stock Market Technical Analysis?**

In order to earn good returns from the stock market, investors need to find reliable, accurate and effective systems to make accurate predictions and remain ahead of market movements. A lot of modern trading systems rely on both stock market technical analysis and fundamental analysis. To be successful in stock market trading, current trading systems are useful to attain the best results. Stock market technical analysis is a method used by experts to predict stock trends. Stock market technical analysis is particularly helpful for long term investors who need accurate and reliable platforms that can guarantee the best results.

Despite the fact that the stock market is volatile, investors and experts with access to the right market information can lower their risks by effectively bracing themselves for future stock movements. This can be achieved by looking at past performance and taking into account earning potentials.

What is stock market technical analysis? This is a technique used to forecast future trends of stock market prices by examining the previous data particularly the prices and volume of shares traded. It's worth mentioning that stock market technical analysis only takes into account the price and volume behavior of stocks. This is because volume and price are the two most important factors that give an indication of how particular stocks will behave in future. Experts who use stock market technical analysis believe that the current price of a stock already carries plenty of information that can be used in determining future investment decisions.

According to stock market technical analysis, external happenings such as news or a high rate of unemployment don't significantly affect the prices of stocks. It's important to point out that technical analysis relies heavily on patterns and charts with an assumption that investors tend to have put forward specific actions and responses.

Despite the fact that a lot of experts and investors find stock market technical analysis a reliable approach, fundamental analysis is also helpful as well. In the case of fundamental analysis, predictions for future stock market prices and stock movements are based on all real and current data. Some of the important considerations that fundamental analysts use to calculate the value of stocks include the overall state of the economy, industry factors such as financial reports and management performance. Other factors include national economic indicators that have a huge impact on what happens in the stock industry.

For those who have very little knowledge about investing in the stock market, the first step is to research thoroughly and find reliable sources of information. A newsletter or an investment guide can provide you with the necessary information and analysis. When looking for expert advice on stock market investing, you should ensure it comes from qualified personnel who have a good grasp of stock market technical analysis and how it can be used to ensure successful stock trading. Professionals tasked with the responsibility of providing advice should also have in-depth knowledge and experience in the stock market.

**What is Technical Analysis?**

Technical analysis is a way of forecasting prices based on prices mathematic calculation in the past. This process involves analyzing the process and charts time series. This method was introduced for gaining profits in stock market, markets of stocks, assets and future markets. Technical analysis methods were formed separately until they became united in the 1970s.

Technical analysis is about forecasting prices by monitoring market movement charts for a period of time. This technique does not consider reasons why prices change but pays attention to the fact that prices are already moving to a specific direction. Technical analysis believes in historic performance of stocks and markets to forecast future performance.

For instance, in a shopping mall, a fundamental analysis was required to visit each store, study each product on sale and decide whether to purchase it or not. On the other hand, a technical analyst would sit on a bench in the mall and watch customers go into the store. When it came to valuing the products in the stores, the technical analyst's decision was based on the patterns or activity of customers going into the store.

The price is considered as the real product price at stock markets or currency index rate. The information that influence product price is considered as the very price and in trade volumes one doesn't need to study price depending on economic, political and other factors. Researching and studying volume dynamics or prices to get information about possible market development is enough. The history of technical analysis indicates that most of the time, prices increase non-interruptedly and this leads to the decrease in bouncing. Since business volume includes both transactions to buy and to sell, fixed price after trade termination doesn't depend on trade volume. The number of transactions and final price are not at any point connected.

Trade volume is the number of positions that are not closed prior the trading day measuring unit for trade volume in national currency. In this case, not all the three technical analysis indicators are the same which means that price is major, followed by volume and lastly open interest. According to the historical facts, price changes reflect on stable psychology of market crowd which means that participants' reaction to the same situations is identical. However, trade volume in combination with price can't change display market demand and offer. The study of trade prices and volume is necessary to gaining experience in realizing transactions at stocks market.  The common rule is following demand and offering set price which is confirmed by volume.

Using technical analysis assists in implicating existence of various axioms. One of the axioms is the market movement in which various factors influencing the price such as economic, psychological and political are considered. The second axiom argues that prices have different directions. The technical analysis aim is to trade determination and making use of three trends; bullish (price rising), bearish (price falling) and sideway (price remains the same). Lastly, the third axiom indicates that history repeats itself.

## What is fundamental analysis?

When it comes to stock trading, understanding the difference between fundamental analysis and technical analysis is important. The difference between these two types of analysis is easy to understand. Fundamental analysis mainly focuses on the economic and company events while technical analysis deals strictly with price action and market behavior. Fundamentals include market share, P/E ratio, earnings report, profits margins, sales, inventories and dividends among others. Technical analysis includes new high/ lows, breakouts, % change and chart patterns among others. In this article, we are going to focus on fundamental analysis.

Fundamental analysis can be simply explained as a way to analyze stocks. For instance, would you accept a job without going through its benefits? If you are required to work overtime, what are the working conditions and how much does it pay? One of the main reasons for taking up a job is to make money, but you want good working conditions to avoid quitting your job. When it comes to investing stocks, you want to do the same thing. The main reason for purchasing stocks is to make money but it's important to carry out enough research to avoid losing your hard-earned money.

The fundamentals of a certain corporation are top priority when looking into stocks not unless you are using technical analysis which uses charts. It's essential to look into the financial statements such as income statement, cash flow statement, balance sheet and regained earnings statement of the corporation. These financial statements will let you know what the corporation owns in assets, their liquidity, how they are doing in terms of cash, how much money they have, how much they owe, where the money goes and more financial information. Although this sounds confusing, analysis of financial statements is an important step in fundamental analysis.

Looking at management is also important. What's the history of the CEO and other management authority? Do they have necessary skills? Have they made any growth in the past? The management of a company can make or break a firm and you need to ensure they are on the right track. Generally, you need to go through the company and decide if they are what they have done in the past because this will help you predict what they can do in future especially in candidate growth. Have you checked their past dividends history? If they pay well and often, they could be perfect for an investor seeking good dividends. Remember to go through their prices and earnings ratio, cash flow and current debt.

The reason of carrying out this complex analysis is to guide you to decide whether you are making the right decision to buy, sell or hold the security of that company. The same type of analysis can be carried out on other securities such as futures, forex, and options. Fundamental analysis can be performed on current and historic data to make a decision. The main aim of doing this is to find the right value of the stock and to try predicting the future growth of the company.

**How to do Fundamental Analysis**
Fundamental and technical analysis are two main methods used for analyzing stock markets. This is important especially if you want to realize profits out of your investment. It's worth mentioning that you can rely on both technical and fundamental analysis to select stocks but only technical analysis is useful when timing the entry and exit of a trade. Fundamental analysis is used by investors to value an investment by comparing its actual value to its equity market value. In case of equity value misplacement, investors are bound to acquire profits. While technical analysis focuses on utilizing charting software to determine past stock patterns, fundamental analysis focuses on the future with an aim of trying to find a firm's true value.

Before doing basic fundamental analysis on stock trends, you need to understand the concepts discussed below and combine them with the use of charts for maximum performance.

Debt to Equity Ratio: A firm's debt to equity ratio is a representation of a company's financial leverage. This ratio is determined by computing a firm's liabilities and dividing them by shareholders' equity. If you realize that a company has a high debt to equity ratio, it implies that the firm has been borrowing a lot in order to finance various business projects. When this happens, it means there are chances for a higher earning potential. However, debt to equity ratio cannot also be determined by various other factors.

Price/Earnings Ratio: This is a critical ratio because it helps one to know the value of a company's stock. This ratio is determined by dividing the share price by the annual EPS (Earnings Per Share). A low price to earnings ratio is an indication that that the stock has been undervalued.

PEG Ratio: Also known as Price to Earning Growth ratio. There is a small difference between PEG Ratio and P/E ratio. This figure is calculated by dividing the P/E ratio by the annual EPS growth value. PEG Ratio is often considered to be an approximation and companies whose PEG Ratio equals to one have a high value.

Cash Flows: Cash Flows come into two forms; either cash flows or Non-operating cash flows. Cash flows refer to the revenue and expenses that are transacted in an account in a specified time period. Cash influx traditionally comes from investing, operations and financing while cash outflow is a detail of expenses. Businesses have records of these financial transactions thanks to accounting statements. The figure is calculated by taking net income after tax deductions and adding it to non-cash charges. Cash flow is important because it shows the strength of a company. Examples of non-operating cash flows include dividend payments, loans, asset sale and other investments.

Earnings Trends: These trends provide useful information because they show a market's movement. Professionals can use this information to ascertain the value of a security. The value of a security can be dictated by economic factors such as interest rates, state of the economy and other indicators.

Once you determine and calculate the above ratios and values, you can use fundamental analysis to identify some of the best stocks as well as have good predictions of stock market trends.

**What is an annual report and why is it useful to investors?**
An annual report can give an investor a lot of useful information about a company. As a regular stockholder, a company sends an investor an annual report. If one is not ready to be a stockholder, one needs to contact the company's shareholder service department and request for a hard copy. One can often view a company's annual report at their website where one can download and print it easily.

As an investor, you need to analyze an annual report to check the following:

You need to know how well a company is doing. Are the earnings lower, higher or the same the previous year? How are the sales doing? These numbers need to be presents clearly in the financial section of the annual report.

You need to find out if the company is making more money that it's spending. How does the balance sheet look? Are the assets higher or lower than the previous year? Is the debt reducing, increasing or stagnant?

You need to have an idea of the management strategic plan for the following year. How will the management team build on the company's success? This plan is covered in the beginning of an annual report.

An investor's task includes figuring out where the company has been, where it is currently and where it is going. As an investor, you do not need to read the annual report like a book ( cover to cover) but instead, approach it like a newspaper and read around to find relevant sections to get answers you need to make a decision whether you should purchase or hold to the stock.

Studies of how many investors read newspaper show different results but a lot suggest that no more than 20% of them get the reports spend any time going through them. Online distribution of corporate paperwork has increased and many investors have been able to find the information they want quickly and easily.

When it comes to annual reports there are some things that an investor needs to look into. Going through the executive summary is essential to know what's going on with the company. You will be surprised of what you find out by just by reading and feeling the tone of the letter. As an investor, you should also look into debt levels, cash on hand, sales and operating profits. You don't need to be an expert to notice year-to-year increase in debt levels or huge decline in sales which is a sign that not all is well.

Go through the brief auditor's report filled with boilerplate. Check for a short note and concentrating that auditors say the statements is accurately representing the company's financial position. In case the management is changing auditors or not agreeing with its accountants, you should wonder if the numbers are trustworthy.  It's also important to check the proxy statements which are included in most annual reports. Annual reports are important because they can help an investor learn more about a company before investing, which is a helpful thing.

## What is listed in an Annual Report?

If you have ever been involved in the process of preparing an annual report, you will agree that it is quite time consuming, requires a lot of concentration and dedication. The process of preparing this report also comes with a budget especially if you have to seek the expertise and input of seasoned professionals. If prepared well, an annual report can be a good marketing tool for a company which in turn, boosts corporate growth.

Customarily, company annual reports usually contain the firm's financial information, balance sheets as well as a report from the chairperson. If firms consider an annual financial report as a firm's marketing plan, it is possible to find unique ways of presenting information in a compelling and useful that includes important pieces of information that can be included to make an annual report reflect on the successes a firm has achieved in the just ended financial period. Doing this is important because at the end of the day, the annual report is read by other people who will use it as a benchmark to measure corporate performance. This report actually forms opinions about a company and clearly portrays the level of financial competence depending on what is contained in your financial report.

So, what is listed in a financial report?

A letter from the chairman of the company: It gives key highlights of the events that shaped the company in the just passed financial year and gives a preview of what is expected to come in the next financial year. Being an annual report, it is important to share with the public what the company has achieved in the previous financial year as well as a sneak preview of what to watch out for going forward. This is critical because it gives both current and potential investors a better understanding of the corporate strategy.

Company philosophy: This is a critical section in any annual report because it gives a detailed account of the principles and ethics that define a company. For investors to gain interest in a company, they need to have a good idea of what the company stands for and believes in. The principles here need to be an eye opener for the outside world.

An extensive report on each section of the company: It is important for any firm to ensure that anyone going through their financial reports understands the products and services that a company deals with.

Financial reports: These reports are critical for any organization because they portray how a company is performing financially. Some of the major financial documents included in an annual report are profit and loss account statements as well as a balance sheet. Depending on the income and expenses, a firm can either make profits or losses within the financial trading period. The balance sheet also gives an account of the assets and liabilities and draws comparisons with the previous years.

Footnotes: Footnotes contain important information such as the current or pending lawsuits. Information included in this section includes government regulations that influence a company's operations.

Auditor's letter: This is an important letter that confirms to everyone going through the annual report that all the data provided in the report is accurate and has been verified and certified by independent accountants.

**How do I obtain an Annual Report?**

An annual report is a publication that public corporations provide to shareholders to explain their operations and financial conditions. The front part of the report usually contains an impressive combination of graphics, pictures and an accompanying narrative. The back part of the report contains detailed financial and operational information.

In case of mutual funds, an annual report is a needed document that is available to fund shareholders on a yearly basis. It shares certain aspects of a fund operations and financial condition. The annual report has become a regular component in corporate financial reporting. Normally, an annual report contains financial highlights, letter to the shareholders, narrative text/graphics/photos, management's discussion & analysis, financial statements, notes to financial statements, auditor's report, summary financial data and corporate information. Mutual fund annual report accompanied with a fund's prospectus and statement of additional information is a source of year fund data and performance which is made available to fund shareholders and potential investors.

Thanks to the internet, finding financial reports has become easier and faster. Today, many reputable companies have investor relations section on their websites that has immense information. For instance, Walt Disney Company is a great example of a business that uses its website to get information from shareholders and investors. If an investor wants to go deeper and beyond the slick marketing version of annual report found on business websites, they will have to search through filings made to the SEC (Securities and Exchange Commission). All companies in the USA that trade publicly are supposed to file regular financial reports with the SEC. These filings include an annual report, quarterly financial reports and a myriad other forms containing various types of financial data.

The reports are uploaded through a system known as Electronic Data Gathering, Analysis and Retrieval System (EDGAR). EDGAR performs an automated collection, indexing, acceptance and forwarding of submissions by companies and other needed by law to file forms with the Securities and Exchange Commission. The info on EDGAR can also be found on SEC website where an investor can search through the forms as well as familiarize himself or herself with the system using a given tutorial.

## Chapter Eleven
## Stock Investing Tips

**What to do when the Market is Down?**

The stock market has its own share of challenges and before investing, you need to realize that it's never a smooth ride in the financial markets. When dramatic movements such as an incident when Dow Jones Industrial Average lost almost 900 points in a single week, it's time to realize that moments will come when things will not be good and you'll be required to make informed decisions. When stock prices begin a depreciating trend, some investors run away from the market and wait for the markets to improve before making a comeback. The only problem is that there is a risk of losing out on recovery stocks that could have brought in good profits.

So, how should you manage your investment when stock markets are going through turbulent times and the prices are low? In most occasions, a lot of investors begin to panic and end up making the wrong decisions. When stock prices slump, it is good to sit back and reflect on your risk tolerance levels. A lot of people venture into stocks without understanding their risk tolerance levels. This is dangerous because the chances of losing an entire investment because of poor decision making are very high. Therefore, you need to be realistic and honest with yourself about the level of losses you're willing to accommodate in a specific timeframe. Carrying out an assessment will help you to determine your portfolio amount you wish to retain.

If you are keen on long term investment, you shouldn't worry about your portfolio so much when stock prices go down because losses can be recovered after some time. When stock markets perform badly and you decide to reduce the percentage of stocks in your portfolio, it further complicates your chances of making your investment dreams come true.

Once you find a risk level you are comfortable with, you can be able to still keep a good amount of stocks that will enable you to attain your investment objectives. If you are focused on building wealth over time and still have many years to retire, you don't need to be worried and take quick decisions when stocks begin to perform below expectations. The most important thing is to ensure your portfolio is aligned with your long-term investment goals together with the level of fluctuation you can comfortably accommodate. In this case, a stock market downturn should be a perfect opportunity for you to purchase more stocks likely to attract high prices.

Another good decision you can take when stock prices drop is to avoid keeping all your eggs in one basket. It is a smart strategy to re-allocate a portion of your assets in stocks to investment ventures which are less risky such as bonds and cash. Significant moves in the stock market can derail you from achieving your financial goals. You should not preoccupy yourself so much from headlines because they derail you from achieving your investment objectives. Learning how to observe the markets and make the right decisions is the only way to succeed as an investor.

**How to avoid common mistakes for beginners like me?**
Making mistakes in life is a part of the learning process. A lot of investors both advanced and newbie have made mistakes in investments. It is not possible to be completely perfect because common investing errors always come up. However, a bigger should avoid common mistakes when it comes to investing.

One of common mistake to look out for is using too much margin. What is margin? This is using borrowed to purchase securities. Margin can assist an investor to make more money but can also exaggerate their losses. Getting carries away with what seem to like free money is a bad thing for investor to entangle himself or herself with. If they use margin and their investment doesn't meet their expectations, they will end up with a large debt obligation all for nothing. Moreover, using margin require an investor to monitor their positions more closely because of exaggerated gains and losses that come with small movements in price.

Buying of unfounded tips is also another mistake to keep an eye on. Most of us assume that everyone makes a mistake at one point in their investing career. You musty heard from friends or relatives discussing about stock that will be bought or have a killer earnings. Although this information may be true, this doesn't mean that the stock is the ideal field that you should hurriedly invest in. Other unfounded tips come from investment professionals on various sources such as TV or radio who often advise on specific stock that is a must buy. These stock tips can at times be misleading and contribute to you failure in stock investing.

An investor should also watch out for day trading mistake. If you decide to become an active trader, you need to be careful on day trading. Day trading is a serious and dangerous game that should only be performed by seasoned investors. Furthermore, a successful day trader need to access special equipment that is not widely available to an average trader.

Buying of stocks that appear cheap is also a common mistake that beginners make when it comes to investing. Those investors who commit this mistake always compare the current share with the week high of stock. A lot people using this method assume that the reduced share price represent a good buy. As an investor, you should avoid purchasing stocks that look like a bargain. In any case there are strong fundamental reasons for a price decline, carry out enough research and analyze the stocks from an honest perspective before investing.

Another common mistake that a beginner goes through is underestimating their abilities. Some investors believe they cannot excel at investing because stocks success is meant for experienced investors. Well, this believe is not true at all because any investor can succeed if they apply the right strategies needed in investment. By devoting enough time to learn and research about stock trading, you will be able equip yourself with enough knowledge to avoid these common mistakes.

### How can I grow my money in the stock market?

Making money is always a dream come true for many investors. Today, there are many investment options available in the market and stock market is one of them. Stock trading can be risky but when done the right way, one can earn a lot of profits. To succeed in stock trading investment, an investor needs to be patience, knowledge and skills needed to succeed. Every investor who invests in stock market wants to learn how the money grows. Your money in stock market grows in two main ways; dividends and increased stock value.

Increased stock value is usually determined by capital appreciation. This capital appreciation is the increase in value of a stock based on the rising market price. The capital increment takes place when the original capital invested in the stock increases in value. In case the stock value increase, an investor cannot earn from it unless they sell their shares. When a firm does not perform as expected due to various factors, the stock price goes down and this is the reason why an investor needs to sell their stock value when it's still high.

Dividends are the other major investment returns paid by a company to its shareholders. Dividends are calculated in terms of the company's revenue. Dividends are usually paid in two forms; stock and cash dividend. Cash dividends are represent the earning offered by the company per stock and stock dividends is the additional stocks offered to the shareholders for free.

An investor needs to have skills and knowledge of stock trading to make money from investment. There are many tips that one can use to grow their money in stock market. Choosing the right strategy to use in stock market is a great way to grow your money. There are different strategies that you can use to invest in stock market. The buy and hold strategy involves buying stocks and holding them to sell them when the market rises. Using this strategy gives you high return from your investment. Another strategy is to time strategy that involves predicting the market and how stocks are likely to trader in the future.

When it comes to stock trading, to grow your money, you need to have patience. This virtue is important if you are keen on making worthwhile profits for your investment in a short period. You have to practice patience in case you lose your investment. Timing the right time to buy and sell your stocks can also help you grow money in stock market. There are specific times when you can purchase stocks and end up not getting any profit. The perfect time to sell or buy your stocks is during recessions.

Before an investor comprehends how their money grows in stock market, they have to understand the factors that influence the value of the prices. These factors can be either internal or external. The internal factors include new service or product and signing of new contracts etc. On the other hand, external factors include foreign exchange, interest rates and inflation among others.

**How will I know I started in the right way?**

Investment is a great way to earn money. When it comes to investing, an investor needs to know the right investment opportunity to venture into. The mistake that many investors make when investing is rushing to invest in opportunities that they are not sure about. This is a wrong move because one can lose a lot of money by putting their money in the wrong places. As investor is supposed to take their time to study the market and learn the right market to invest in. Taking enough time to learn and understand the market is a great idea to kick off a successful investing. This knowledge and skills comes in handy when you have to make the right decision to grow your money. There is nothing as frustrating as investing your hard earned money on an investment and losing all of it.

To succeed in investing, you need to start your investing career the right way. You need to know what to expect in the investment world, what to do and not to do. Nowadays, there is a lot of information about market investment that can guide both an advanced and newbie investor. The way you start your investing path determines whether you will succeed or not. Instead of jumping into an investment without second thoughts, take your time to understand what you are getting into to be able to earn money back. An investor should always take investment serious because their money is involved and their main goal is to make money not lose it.

When a new investor decides to venture into stock trading, they need to learn some of the best investments. To know you are on the right tract on stock market as a beginner, you should invest in index fund and ETFs because they present the best opportunity to diversify and reduce risk while you stay investing in markets high or low. Having a well-designed investment portfolio can neither go higher with equities nor crash to earth with corrections. You can also sell off as stock rises and reinvest when prices fall using new cash, interest inflows and dividends.

Since a lot of investors are not retiring tomorrow or anytime sooner, they tend to trade with their retirement account. This is a huge mistake because you should never use your retirement account to trade in stock. An investor can get steady by compounding return that investment experts seek and you can do it yourself at minimal cost and risk. All it takes to make money in investment is to take a broad view of opportunities in the market and patience to see succeed in the end.

**When is the Stock Market Open?**

For any investor who has put their money into the stock market, information about when stock markets open and close will be useful for you. Traditionally, most U.S. financial markets open from Mondays to Fridays from 9.00 am to 4.00 pm. It is important to note that financial markets remain closed over the weekend and during public holidays. Information about trading times is important for traders who need to enter the market and execute the appropriate transactions.

However, the introduction of online trading thanks to the emerging technologies has introduced a whole new spectrum of trading. Having online trading accounts has made it possible for a lot of traders to trade round the clock way after the official closing times. In this day and age, a lot of countries are embracing 24 hour economies and it is expected that the financial markets will too be part of this initiative. Due to the increasing number of day traders who are earning a living from stock markets, there has been a lot of increased activity in the financial markets.

The emergence of the internet has made it easier and more convenient for traders to comfortably carry out their trades from remote locations. Long gone are the days when you were required to be physically present at stock market trading floors. Nowadays, with the click of a button, you can comfortably be able to initiate transactions at any time of the day and night. This is important because even after stock markets have officially closed for the day, a lot of market events that affect stock prices still go on outside the official working hours.

Knowing the timings of stock markets is important because you can use this to your advantage and determine the best times to initiate transactions. There are certain periods during trading times when there are changes in stock movements. Any good investor should keep an eye on the market and learn to observe the markets in order to make the appropriate decisions. Technology has introduced a lot of changes especially when it comes to trading times.

### How Much Return can I Expect?

We all invest in the stock market with the hope of getting good returns. However, before committing your money for investment, it is always good to have a thorough knowledge of the available market trends in order to make good decisions. It's worth mentioning that the rates of returns differ depending on the type of securities that you have invested in. Before embarking on an investment, knowing what the anticipated return is always important because based on this information you can decide whether you want to invest or not.

It is known that the level of risk is directly proportional to the returns that an investor gets. This means that high risk investments that keep you on the edge of your seat are actually the best in terms of return of investment. So, if you are keen on realizing better returns, you might be compelled to go for high risk investments with a full understanding of your risk profile and how much losses you are willing to suffer in case of market downturns. On the other hand, low risk investments are ideal for those who are not ready to invest in high risk ventures. However, the return obtained is usually not very high.

This means that before determining the type of returns you want to achieve from your investment, you need to be very honest about how much risk you are willing to take. This is important because it determines whether you will select a low, medium or high risk investment. Knowing what type of securities trade under each category is essential for purposes of good decision making. Prior to investing, it is wise to consult a qualified financial expert who can advise you regarding the various investment options which are available.

There are platforms that offer guidelines in terms of the rates of returns for different types of securities. Taking time to go through this information is important because you can have a good idea of what you will get from your investment. One to note however is that returns do not come automatically. Just because you have been told that a particular stock has a 20% per annum return on investment means this will always be the case. There are several factors that influence stock prices and at times, the markets can take unexpected turns and instead, you end up making losses.

Knowing the expected return on investment is essential because it gives you the motivation to continue investing knowing that your efforts are not going to waste. In summary, different types of investment ventures come with their own anticipated rates of returns. Before investing, take time to examine the rates and choose an investment plan will meet both your preferences and expectations.

**How Do I Know which Stocks to Buy?**

The stock market is a common investment channel for many investors looking to make more money to improve their financial positions. Given the fact that there are several stocks to choose from, making the right decision can at times be challenging. However, with thorough market research and use of accurate industry information, the process of choosing the most ideal stocks shouldn't be so much of a hassle.

If you are planning to purchase stocks, you will realize that there are different techniques that claim to give the most accurate outcome for stock picking. It's worth mentioning that taking caution is important because there is no 100% fool-proof methods that assure you success on the best stock picks. There are several proposals that have been put forward that investors can use to determine the right stocks to invest in.

Fundamental analysis is one of the most credible methodologies that you can use to choose stocks. Going through the information contained in this analysis is important but you should note that they are not all foolproof. The good news is that you don't need to rely on fundamental analysis alone to choose your stocks, there are other techniques and factors that can guide you to making the right decision.

Stock market indexes have thousands of companies and knowing the best company to choose can be very challenging. Having a plan before beginning the selection process will save you a lot of trouble. The selection criteria for long term and short term investors should not be the same.

The health of a firm depends on its management team. How a company performs entirely depends on how competent the management team is and what experience do they have in the specific industry sector a company is trading. Evaluating how managers have performed in their previous assignments is a good hint of how they will perform in the current role.

Check the sector the company is in. Remember that how a company performs is determined by the condition of the sector. In order for a company to post good results, it is critical for the overall sector to be experiencing positive growth. A company performing well in an industry sector that is struggling is risky because chances are high that a firm's performance will eventually be compromised. If the stock you intend to invest in comes from a sector that is performing dismally, it will be wise not to put your money into the industry.

Demand and supply are both critical factors that speak volumes about a company's performance. Going back to technical analysis, a lot of investors use this technique because it gives a clearer and more accurate picture of supply and demand in reference to trading volumes, price studies and investor trends in stock. Information obtained from these studies is more useful for predicting short term to medium term trends. If you are keen with long term predictions, consider analyzing other technical indicators such as relative strength index, money flow index, stochastics and MACD (Moving Average Convergence/Divergence).

**How Can I Track Stocks?**

Due to the high cost of living and financial pressure, a lot of people are looking for extra ways to invest and make money. Nowadays, everyone is interested in making more money and stock trading is one of the best platforms to invest. However, before investing in stocks, there are essential guidelines that every investor needs to know. If you want to become an aggressive stock market trader, you need to be familiar with the tools and techniques that will enable you to keep track of stock prices. The key to becoming a successful stock market trader is to learn how to keep an eye on stock prices and make the appropriate decisions. Without an effective and accurate stock tracking platform, it becomes difficult to determine whether you're making profits or losses.

Many people who have not ventured into stocks have realized that a lot of investors have been using stocks to generate wealth and gather capital which is later used for other investments. In the earlier days, tracking of stock markets was by use of manual approaches. However, in the recent times, emerging technologies and the internet have completely transformed the entire stock market industry. Nowadays, there are several automated systems and platforms that you can use to track stocks. Stock analysis is an important exercise for any investor because it gives you the heads up on what is happening in the industry.

If you have a keen interest of being control of your money and you're unsure of which are the right stocks to keep to attain your investment goals, you need to educate yourself about how to track and analyze stock markets in order to accurately and effectively interpret price fluctuations. Before investing in stocks, you should know that embracing the right stock tracking tools is essential because as an investor, you must be constantly updated on current happenings and how they're affecting stock prices. Remember that when stock prices fluctuate, they price could either increase or decrease. Having accurate and real-time reporting tracking tools is important because you can be able to make decisions depending on the current market circumstances.

Technical analysis the habit of constantly monitoring stock market charts and trends to keep track of movements in price as they happen over time. Having knowledge of tracking stocks is not as difficult as many people think. Nowadays, there are several systems that will practically do for you everything and avail information and data that will facilitate good decision making. A lot of investors are using online tracking platforms to see how stock prices are fluctuating. The advantage is that many of these platforms offer real-time alerts either through mobile alerts and emails. In the recent times, a lot of Apps have been designed to integrate with mobile platforms so that investors still receive alerts while on the move.

The media is also instrumental in helping investors to track their stocks. Most media platforms have regular stock market updates to inform both investors and the general public about what is happening in the industry.

## How to Make Money in Stocks

Nowadays, a lot of people are looking for ways to make an extra income. Everyone is looking for a way to grow their investments in order to secure a better financial future. With the rising economic crisis across the globe, a lot of people have been forced to look for alternative ways to secure their financial freedom. If you have a family, it is imperative that you find other ways to secure your income outside your normal job description. Money is an essential commodity that everyone is looking for in order to protect their loved ones.

These days, it is not enough to have plenty of money. A good investor should not keep money but rather, find ways of how to grow it. Some people prefer to keep money in a fixed deposit account which is not the best idea because the chances of expanding your investment are small. For a long period of time, investing in the stock market has been used by many people as a way of growing income over a period of time. With the right strategies, investing in the stock markets is a very rewarding venture. Some people who end up becoming stock traders lose their savings because they fail to follow the right protocols and procedures. Lack of accurate information is the main reason why some investors lose their money in stocks.

To be a successful stock broker, you need to take time and understand what goes on in the stock market and commodities market. A lot of people fail to pay attention to the basics which is a big mistake as an investor. The first step of making money from stocks is to choose to invest in the right company with great financial prospects. When you purchase stocks with the lowest price tag, chances of making profits are high especially with speculative stocks.

To have a good understanding of stock market dynamics, trying out mock stock sales is an excellent way to test the waters. You can pick your favorite stocks and monitor their prices to see how they are responding to various market trends. Using this analysis, you should try and find out if your extrapolations are working as they should. Practicing is a good way of gaining experience and learning to react to different circumstances.

Talking to experts and learning from their experience gives you the best opportunity to learn more about the basics of the stock market. Investing in stocks is a decision you should only take after you have done careful research and found a professional and well experienced stock broker. To maximize your profits, it's good to trade with safer stocks and stay away dangerous and volatile stocks especially if you're not prepared to incur high risks.

There are several success stories of people who have become millionaires thanks to investing in stocks. As an investor, it is your personal responsibility to research and equip yourself with information you need to trade effectively.

**What is the best single saving tip?**
Nowadays, many people are open to saving for the future. There are so many ways that a trader or investor can adapt to make incredible savings. Many people who save for a rainy day can agree that this money comes in handy. However, one is the biggest barrier to saving is not having the habit of saving and the best way to get into this habit is to pay yourself first. Having money directly deposited from your checking account into your dedicated savings account can be done at the same time with other goals such as paying a debt. Putting your savings on autopilot is a good way to reinforce savings having especially when unplanned expenses come along and take what you had saved.

During a rainy day, you want to have enough money when you need it which should be free of investment risk. Using the wrong checking account can take your hard-earned money out of your pocket every year. The normal interesting checking account charges a small amount of money and required maintaining a balance. Always look for an account that charges no monthly service fees or per transaction fees and does not require a minimum balance. The majority of banks and credit unions can waive the fee for customers with many account relationships. You need to check out bank tips to avoid fees and use the net to find a free checking account that meets your needs.

Tracking your spending; daily, weekly or monthly is very important. This is the best single saving tip that can help you save a lot of money. Whether you are using a budget or a spending plan, keeping track of your spending can help you to determine where you can cut back and assist you to maximize your saving efforts. Try as much as possible to track your spending for a long period and use this information to come up with a realistic monthly budget. Every month, track all of your expenses from $1 tip of grocery store to your monthly mortgage payment. At the end of the month, tally your spending against your budget and see where you did well and wrong. If you spent less than you had planned, move the extra to your saving account or use it to pay an existing debt.

For many people, another great return on their money is to pay down credit card debt. Whether you are carrying any balances, credit card debt is the most expensive debt. Adding excess money into paying off credit card debt is a risky free return because it lowers the existing balance and resulting interest charges. A consumer with a strong credit profile can find interest rates at lower percentage offer.  When planning a debt repayment, it's good to start with the highest rate card and pay attention on paying off the balances in descending order. You can also use a debt pay down calculator to develop a month-by-month plan for paying off your debt.

**What are some of the Tips of Growing Money on the Stock Market?** The stock market is known to be one of the most popular ways of investing. Everyone who joins the stock market anticipates making profits. The secret of growing your money through the stock market is to come up with tips that will ensure you make well-timed and wise decisions that will see your investment portfolio expand.

If you're keen on getting into stock trading, you need to come up with a proper plan and determine how much you're willing to comfortably invest. The most important thing that you need to do is avoid investing more funds than you can afford to lose. The stock market is lucrative but without proper planning and wise decision making, you can lose your entire investment.

Below are critical tips that you need to survive and make money on the stock market:

Evaluate all your decisions: The stock market has turned around the lives of many. However, not everyone makes money and becomes rich with stock markets. In order to obtain good results, you must invest your time and be very keen with details in order to make profits. Every decision you make in stock trading has consequences and therefore, it is important to think through before making any critical trading decisions. It's also good to be realistic and understand that you cannot be a millionaire overnight. Don't make a mistake of quitting your daytime job for day trading until you are absolutely sure about your decision.

Research and plan: If you are planning to invest money in stocks or any other investment, you need to be fully aware of what is happening in the market. In order to become successful, you must learn how to interpret market trends, prices as well as factors that have a direct impact on the stock market. Before you select a company to invest in, do a thorough background check and try and learn as much as possible about the company. Having a prospectus and knowledge of market trends is a good way to begin trading on the stock market.

Don't get emotional: Success in stock markets comes when you learn how to be cool headed in order to get things done. Becoming emotional is detrimental because it derails you off the right path towards achieving investment success. Furthermore, you should be reasonable and make decisions that will contribute towards the growth of your investment portfolio. For instance, you cannot afford to hold onto a stock whose price is depreciating on a daily basis. When you notice things aren't going as you expected, it's time to make hard decisions in order to save your fortune. It's always better to get out than lose everything you have worked so hard for.

Get the right information: Successful stock trading depends on the decisions you make. In this business, you cannot afford to obtain information from unreliable sources. Getting word from the street, relatives, friends or even business associates is not a wise idea. This means that you need to be extremely cautious especially when obtaining information. A good way to get accurate information is to sign up for alerts from reputable stock trading platforms in order to obtain real-time news and alerts to facilitate better decision making. In case you get a tip from someone, it's always good to do your due diligence and find out the truth.

Market management skills: To be a successful trader, you must know how to trade effectively in both a rising and falling market. Doing this is very important because when stock prices begin to depreciate, you won't panic but will instead calmly come up with good ideas and look for alternative strategies to obtain the best profits.

Money management: In order to achieve good profits, you must learn how to manage your money and try as much as possible to prevent risks that jeopardize your investment. You cannot be a successful stock trader without good money management skills. This is because you need to devise strategies of how to invest, use your profits wisely and reinvest in order to expand your investment portfolio.

In summary, stock trading should not be considered as a get rich quick scheme. If you intend to become a stock trader, you must learn how to grow your investment and keep risks at bay.

## What is the best single saving tip?

Nowadays, many people are open to saving for the future. There are so many ways that a trader or investor can adapt to make incredible savings. Many people who save for a rainy day can agree that this money comes in handy. However, one is the biggest barrier to saving is not having the habit of saving and the best way to get into this habit is to pay yourself first. Having money directly deposited from your checking account into your dedicated savings account can be done at the same time with other goals such as paying a debt. Putting your savings on autopilot is a good way to reinforce savings having especially when unplanned expenses come along and take what you had saved.

During a rainy day, you want to have enough money when you need it which should be free of investment risk. Using the wrong checking account can take your hard-earned money out of your pocket every year. The normal interesting checking account charges a small amount of money and required maintaining a balance. Always look for an account that charges no monthly service fees or per transaction fees and does not require a minimum balance.

The majority of banks and credit unions can waive the fee for customers with many account relationships. You need to check out bank tips to avoid fees and use the net to find a free checking account that meets your needs.

Tracking your spending; daily, weekly or monthly is very important. This is the best single saving tip that can help you save a lot of money. Whether you are using a budget or a spending plan, keeping track of your spending can help you to determine where you can cut back and assist you to maximize your saving efforts. Try as much as possible to track your spending for a long period and use this information to come up with a realistic monthly budget. Every month, track all of your expenses from $1 tip of grocery store to your monthly mortgage payment. At the end of the month, tally your spending against your budget and see where you did well and wrong. If you spent less than you had planned, move the extra to your saving account or use it to pay an existing debt.

For many people, another great return on their money is to pay down credit card debt. Whether you are carrying any balances, credit card debt is the most expensive debt. Adding excess money into paying off credit card debt is a risky free return because it lowers the existing balance and resulting interest charges. A consumer with a strong credit profile can find interest rates at lower percentage offer. When planning a debt repayment, it's good to start with the highest rate card and pay attention on paying off the balances in descending order. You can also use a debt pay down calculator to develop a month-by-month plan for paying off your debt.

**What are the basic steps in managing my money?**
We are living in hard economic times and it's important for you to know how to take care of your hard earned cash. There are several circumstances that

we come across that can derail us from the goal of effectively managing our finances. When it comes to money management, there are things you should and shouldn't do in order to ensure that you develop good savings habits. The steps below are guidelines that you can use to ensure that you adopt good money management skills that will play a critical role in shaping your financial future.

Know when to stop: A lot of people fail to acquire good money management skills because they don't have an idea when to stop. Having a clear idea when you should cease using your money is directly related to the different aspects of your finances. Budgeting is a critical skills that you need to have because it enables you to know your daily, weekly and monthly budgets. You need to understand at which level you should stop investing in one financial portfolio and dwell on another. For instance, this means you must know when to stop using credit cards and instead, purchase with real money. These 'stops' are critical for an individual's financial success because you have to suffer some inconveniences in order to know where you need to stop. If you are paying too much for luxuries, you need to be ready to undergo some inconveniences in order to know where to stop.

Eliminate Impulse Buys: A lot of people fail to realize their financial targets because of impulse buying. The truth is that most stores in business rely on impulse purchases and you can be easily drawn into buying items you had not planned for. When you get into a store and end up purchasing items that you had not planned, you end up spending money meant for something else or saving. Learning to stick to your budget is very important because this way, you are able to stay within your financial means.

Learn how to plan ahead: You can never be successful with money management if you lack planning skills. When you have no elaborate plan of how you intend to spend your money, chances are high that you will not have if after a couple of weeks. Planning ahead is important because it helps you to identify your priorities well in advance and allocate the required finances.

Summary of money management steps
Step 1: Know your total sum of monthly expenses and set it aside from your paycheck. Such expenses include rent, cable payments, water, electricity etc.

Step 2: Decide on an amount you will be saving every week. Put it aside in an emergency fund. Don't choose a very large amount. Choose a small figure you can comfortably part with.

Step 3: Come with a meal plan and do advance grocery shopping. Having enough food will ensure that you don't keep going back to the store every time you are in town.

Step 4: Weekly spending you should never exceed 10% of your paycheck. If you overspend, you shouldn't pick more money to avoid dipping into the week's budget.

Step 5: Set your financial goals. If you want to gain financial freedom, it is important to set goals that will come true. Finances are tricky and in order to save, you have to make it happen. By doing this, you will be able to know how to manage your money and get on track towards becoming financially independent.

A lot of people think that managing money is difficult yet it is not. If you are committed about buying your dream house or saving for retirement, you need to know what is adequate when it comes to spending. Controlling or stopping impulse purchases coupled with good financial planning will definitely enable you to manage your money better. You should know that financial planning is not rocket science and anyone can save. Do not use an excuse of earning little money not to save because learning how to live within your means regardless of what you earn is the best way to secure financial freedom.

## How can I stop my Bad Saving Habit?

Do you work so hard yet you don't see any financial gains? A lot of people agree that this unfortunate scenario is real and happens to them. Saving is a simple term yet many people have been unable to save their way to financial freedom despite having good income streams. You need to realize that without putting aside extra money, you can never be able to achieve anything substantial without developing a skill of saving. It takes a lot of discipline to gain momentum in financial savings.

Don't spend all your money: This habit is the most dangerous habit that prevents you from saving money to use on other useful ventures that will improve your financial capability. The most important thing you need to do to get away from bad habits that prevent you from saving is to learn how to budget for your money and stop spending all the money you have. Never consider using your savings on other issues other than agreeable and profitable ventures. When you spend your money carelessly, you are often forced to dig into your savings which is a dangerous habit that compromises your chances of saving. It is also wise to avoid spending more than 50% of money that you have carried with you.

Do not waste your money on expensive items: Instead of going around and spending your money on pricey items that don't add value, keep your savings and think about making your retirement better. When you are broke with no money, you have to go through the inconvenience of not having certain items in your life. If you can cut out luxuries when you are financially broke, why would you then need to purchase them when you have money? Believe it or not, there are many people out there who lead comfortable life without having to spend excessively on unnecessary purchase that cost a lot of money to acquire.

If you must spend money on expensive items, ensure that you don't repeat this habit because it amounts to financial suicide. Remember that it is your will and choice to shop extravagantly and having financial discipline does not mean you should be stingy, you just need to careful and know what is good for you. If you must purchase expensive items, don't be in a hurry. Instead, find places where there are discounts in order to make good savings. When shopping, you just need to focus on what you want and avoid spending your money on unnecessary items.

When you spend money wisely, you have a good opportunity of increase your money and have enough to focus on other investment ventures that will be beneficial to you in the long run.

## What Are Some of the Tips on Money Management?

With proper planning and discipline, you can use the little available financial resources you have to better your financial future. Money management is a contentious topic that affects many people desperately looking for ways to manage their money properly. The following are some of the tips you can use to achieve better and efficient use of money.

Come up with a budget: Before coming up with a schedule of how to manage your money, you need to come up with a realistic weekly, monthly and yearly budget. When coming up with a budget, it needs to have both your income and expenses. Expenses should include the full amount details as well as the description of the expense. Next, try to allocate 10% of your income to savings since you have already determined how much you need for paying bills and other expenses.

Shop carefully: A lot of people fail to realize their financial aspirations because of careless spending. It is always good to make sure that you shop responsibly without having to overspend. When you have a budget, you have a guide that you can refer to when shopping to avoid impulse buying. When you are out shopping and you spot something exciting you wish to purchase, you must look at the price tag and make reference to your budget to see if you can afford. People who have managed to spend wisely have realized a lot of successes when it comes to money management. Actually, this is the most important money management tip.

Avoid credit: Debt is not good especially if you are looking towards become a good money manager. Credit is a derailment from money management because borrowing funds is directly the opposite of money planning. You can never be a good financial planner when you are involved with a lot of debt. Credit cards are particularly risky because they entice many individuals to spend beyond what they can comfortably afford.

Reduce on other unnecessary expenditures: Drawing up plans of efficient money management is an exercise in futility so long as you don't cut down on some expenses. Achieving financial goals usually comes with some commitments for instance, reducing the number of times you use your car and instead, opt for public means or use pool car to commute to the office. Frequent expensive lunches and dinners should also be minimized. This way, you can be able to maximize on unspent cash which can then be channeled into useful ventures.

Monitor and track your expenses: If you want to see where your money is going and take the appropriate action to curb wasteful spending, you must put in place mechanisms that monitor how you're spending your finances. When you monitor your expenses, you will have a better idea of cash outflow and how to implement measures that will encourage efficient money management.

Look for alternative income channels: When you increase your income streams, you have more money at your disposal and therefore, you can easily plan your finances. We are living in financial turbulent times where one source of income might not be adequate to meet all your financial expectations. Alternative income is good because it supplements your regular income which in turn, makes life more comfortable.

**Is the Stock Market Good for Retirement Investing?**

Nowadays, a lot of people are looking for ways to save for retirement. Considering the current high cost of living and rapidly changing economic times, it is important for investors to begin looking at ways of securing their finances at old age. Nowadays, there are several ways to save for the future. However, investing in stocks is one of the most common options that several people opt for. Thanks to stock investments, a lot of individuals have been able to expand their financial investment portfolios and in turn, lived a financially independent life.

People invest in stocks for different reasons. If you decide to purchase stocks for retirement purposes, it is always better to do it when you're still young. The stock market is highly volatile and early investment gives you plenty of time to expand your investment portfolio. When choosing stocks for retirement purposes, it is essential to carefully research and get all your facts before making any decisions. Investing in stocks for retirement means it's a long term investment and therefore, you must choose to invest in firms which are stable in terms of financial performance.

When planning to invest in stocks for retirement, you need to understand the level of risk involved. Since you're investing for long periods of time, chances are high your stocks will be faced with ups and downs. Understanding the level of risk involved is important because this way, you can be able to decide early enough if you are really prepared to face the challenges that come with long term stock investing.

In order to realize maximum benefits when investing in stocks, it is important to diversify your investment portfolio. Unlike individuals who are interested in short term gains, your strategy should be to carefully examine the market and come up with a list of top performing companies which have managed to successfully keep their stocks on the profitable side. For long-term investors, it is wise to spread your investment across several companies. By doing this, you are assured that in case stocks of one company don't perform well, you still stand a good chance of recouping your investment and earning good profits.

Retirement investment has to be approached with caution especially when dealing with stock investments. Before putting your money into any company, it is important to have extensive consultations with retirement financial experts on which approach to use for investing in stocks. Remember that the strategies used for long term and short term investing are not the same. The good news is that there are plenty of retirement planning experts with knowledge of how to invest in the stock market and reap good benefits. Getting the right set of advice from qualified experts is the best way to know how to approach retirement planning.

Retirement investing is a wise thing to do especially if you want to live a fruitful life of financial abundance. However, before putting your money into stock, have your goals clearly defined and speak to an expert.

**How Much Do You Need to Buy Shares of a Company?**
How much do I need to purchase stocks in a company? This is a question that many people ask themselves. In order to know how much you want to spend, there are some guiding factors that should be used to enable you make an informed decision. The stakes are high in the stock market and therefore, it is crucial to have a clear understanding of your goals before deciding how much you want to invest. In order to determine how much

investment you require in the stock market, you first need to know the type of stocks you intend to purchase. Remember that different types of stocks have varying market values.

Investing in common stocks is an investment many people opt to go for. When you purchase stocks in a company, you become an official shareholder and have the right to vote at shareholder meetings. Different types of companies have common stocks that sell at different prices. Alternatively, you can choose to go for preferred stocks that offer you limited company ownership. Preferred stocks generate a higher yield compared to common stocks and therefore, you might be forced to pay more for them. Penny stocks are commonly associated with small companies and are usually priced at $5 per share.

Before buying company shares, you need to have come up with a budget of how much you intend to invest in stocks. It is impossible to give an exact amount required to become a stock trader because various factors determine this decision. You should know that the price of a stock depends on how a company is performing. When you decide to buy stocks in companies which are performing well, be prepared to pay more for stock prices.

The amount of money you spent on purchasing stocks depends on the time you decide to invest. When it comes to the time to invest, there are many current prevailing factors that cause price fluctuations. This means that the time you decide to venture into the financial market is very important. Also, you need to have a clear plan of how long you intend to remain active in the stock market.

The amount of shares you are planning to buy obviously affects stocks prices. For those who are keen to invest heavily, it will require one to purchase a higher volume of stocks which will demand more money to be spent on investment. For new investors, it is always advisable to spend less and learn about the stock market business before putting in more money.

The amount of money to be spent on buying stocks should be decided only after careful planning, knowing how much you want to spend and your investment objectives. Even if you have a lot of money, you shouldn't be in a hurry to invest the entire amount without having a plan of how to take care of your investment. The internet has plenty of information in case you need to find out how much you need to begin with.

**Aside from reading, what else do I need?**
Investing in the stock market is a rewarding venture that can reap good benefits if careful planning is done. If you want to invest in financial securities, you must be a good reader because there is a lot of information that you use in order to make wise investment decisions. Unfortunately, some investors wish to reap good profits from investing in the financial markets but fail because of lack of knowledge that leads to wrong decision making. Once you know how to read and find useful information that can assist you in your trade, you need to other tools to ensure that your trading is successful.

Since we are living in the era of technology, it is important for you to ensure that you move with the times and incorporate technology into your trading activities. Nowadays, the internet has facilitated an easier way for traders to trade in a convenient and satisfactory manner. These days, having an online trading account is the newest trend in the securities market as investors can conveniently and easily set up their internet trading accounts. A lot of things happen that affect the movement of stock markets and therefore, it is important to subscribe with platforms that give you real-time updates and information regarding the stock market.

A good stock trading experience is only achievable if you work with a reputable stock trader. It is important to mention that choosing a professional stock trader is the first step of the journey towards successful financial investment. By working with a qualified and reputable stock broker, you are assured that they will provide you with all the technical assistance you required to get started with trading. Using the internet is a good way to identify the best stock brokers because you can read reviews and determine who offers the best service.

Having a good trade plan is essential before you get into any stock trading market. A trading plan gives you a guideline of how you are supposed to enter and exit trade. With a good blueprint, you are assured that you will be safeguarded from losses that you cannot be able to recover from. There is an option of coming up with your own trading plan or use plans that have been devised by other traders so long as they in sync with your personality. You should make sure that the risks and policies outlined in the trading plan match with your preferences.

Any trader who is serious about making profits must invest in the right charting software. These applications not only help you to design charts but also assist you to do technical analysis of data. For instance, you can chart instance to check out thousands of securities and select the ones that you like.

Back Testing Tool: Using this tool, you can check if your plan will work well based on the historical data. Having this tool is important because it prevents you from unexpected losses. If your plan works perfectly fine with past data, chances are high it will perform well in the current conditions.

Choosing a data provider is one of the crucial decisions you have to make. When choosing, make sure to go for a provider that accommodates and offers support for multiple markets. Also, ensure they avail quick download speeds and do regular database checks. A good provider should have a reputable track history in service delivery and performance.

With the above tools in place, you are now ready to begin stock trading with the assurance that you have everything that you need to make good decisions in order to reap financial gains.

**Can I Retire a Millionaire?**

In life, we go through different stages. Retirement is a notable period in any individual's life because it is that this time that you reflect on your past successes and look forward to a relaxing and enjoyable retirement. However, to achieve this, you need to ensure that you begin making good financial decisions when you are still young. A comfortable retirement is achievable if there is good planning and sound money management policies. Retirement marks the beginning of a period when you are no longer in active employment. In order to be successful, retirement planning needs to begin early to guarantee both financial and personal comfort during retirement.

It is always everyone's wish to retire comfortably but having a retirement plan which will work well with your financial expectations is the most challenging part. The good news is that having a good retirement plan is not as difficult as we may think. A lot of people who live a comfortable retirement life are beneficiaries of a direct retirement plan.

So, what is retirement planning? This is the process of determining how you will survive financially after you quit active employment. Retirement planning entails computing expenses, income evaluation and using financial saving programs. It is important to mention that making plans for your retirement does not only involve finances but also includes other personal matters as well. Personal choices associated with retirement include lifestyle choices, how to use your time during retirement and the best time to retire.

You can retire a millionaire and live a comfortable life if you begin making plans for retirement early enough. When most of us hear about retirement, a lot of us think about old age. The mistake is that if you fail to make adequate plans in good time, old age will catch up with you so fast. Beginning to invest when you're still young and allowing time for your investment to grow is the surest way to accumulate wealth. When you begin early, you save money more because late retirement plans are usually costly.

Effective planning: In life, every decision whether large or small has to be planned for. When you plan early, you avoid making future mistakes that can be a threat to your investment. Planning for retirement has helped a lot of people make savings and investment that have enabled them to realize huge financial gains and have an incredibly huge amount of wealth.

Seek expert advice: As much as retirement planning requires a lot of work from your side, getting a professional to advice you on how to invest money and create wealth is beneficial. The advantage of using an expert is they help you make wise choices regarding financial matters that have a direct impact on your retirement. Furthermore, a professional can guide you, track your investments and let you know whether you need to take any decisions or expand your investment portfolio.

Be disciplined: If you want to be a millionaire at retirement, you must cut down on expenses that don't add any value to your financial portfolio. Financial discipline is a critical virtue for anyone who is looking forward to living a luxurious life at retirement.

Retirement planning is an ongoing process that requires dedication, discipline, focus and result oriented to get the final payoff. Only those who are truly committed to this cause get to reap the benefits. If you envision yourself to be a millionaire when you retire, the time to work and invest is now. Do not wait any longer and yes, you can be a millionaire at you retire!

**Will Somebody Always Buy my Stocks when I Sell them?**

 Whenever you are in the stock market business, you must be ready to buy and sell stocks. There comes a time in the stock market business when you need to dispose of your stocks with the aim of either converting your investment into cash or sourcing for extra funds to buy more stocks. If you want to sell your stocks, you shouldn't worry because there always will be a buyer to purchase them. Remember that traders have different trading cycles and therefore, when you plan to sell stocks, there are traders on the other hand who are looking for stops to purchase so that they can enter the market.

The first step is to contact your broker to notify them of your intention to sell your stocks. Alternatively, if you are using an online trading account, you can place an order using your online brokerage account. This is just the first step of the selling process. Next, your broker should then forward your sell order to a market center for purposes of execution. Trade execution refers to the process of filling your order. When your broker receives your request, they have a variety of options they can use to execute your trade.

Exchange: An exchange refers to a marketplace where traders come to either buy or sell both their stocks and bonds. Once a stock is listed on a stock exchange, your broker can ensure orders are directed to that exchange, another exchange or a market maker.

Market Maker: This is a company that is always on standby and ready to sell or purchase stocks at publicly quoted prices. In a bid to get orders from brokers, some market makers will make payments to brokers who direct orders to them. This scenario is referred to as 'payment for order flow'. In the case of stocks that trade in an OTC (over-the-counter) market, your broker is responsible for sending your order to an OTC market maker. It's worth mentioning that OTC market makers also make payments to brokers to secure order flows.

ECN (Electronic Communications Network): One good way of selling your stocks is directing your order to an ECN. An Electronic Communications Network is an electronic based trading system that matches both buy and sell orders at specified prices. This system operates electronically and is very efficient. With an ECN, you are guaranteed that your sell order will be matched with buy orders.

Internalization: Internalization is whereby your broker directs your order to a division of a broker's firm in order for it to be filled out in the firm's inventory. By doing this, your broker can make some profits 'spread' which is the difference between the what the firm paid to buy the security and the price it sells it you.

Using some of the above methods accompanied with selecting a good broker, you can be assured that the process of selling your stocks will be smooth and efficient.

**What are the main ways to make money with stocks?**

Nowadays, a lot of people are investing in the stock market because of the chances of getting good returns. If you are wondering 'how can I make money from the stock market?' you don't need to worry so long as you employ the right strategies. The major question that people ask is how does one earn good returns from the stock market? The first step of obtaining good returns from selling shares and stocks is to first know how to identify the best and most lucrative stocks. The good news is that there are different ways that you can get handsome returns from the stock market.

Buy low, sell high, dividends, option trading and futures are some of the ways that investors can use to earn money from the stock market. However, the two most common ways that investors use to earn money from the stock market is through dividends or to buy low stock and sell high. A lot of investors have successfully managed to earn good returns from stocks thanks to employing good trading strategies. It is important to mention that there are many factors that contribute to how you earn from stocks.

To begin with, you need to find a good company to invest your money in. identifying the ideal company is not challenging as many people think. There are always several market indicators that can show you a company is performing well. Should you realize that a company has a positive growth trend, this is a good of knowing a top performing company. Going back to see how a firm has performed in the previous years is useful because it gives you a clearer picture of a firm's ratings.

Buy low and sell high is a common technique used by many investors to earn money. Just like any other investment venture, your plan should be to invest money and work towards maximizing your profits. In this technique, investors watch the markets and enter when stock prices are trading at low prices. The best strategy is to invest in a bear market when prices are on a depreciating trend and sell stocks in a bullish market. Your ultimate aim should be to reap as much profit as possible.

Secondly, when you invest in a good company, chances are high it will perform well in the stock market. When a firm records impressive performance and obtains good returns, shareholders always receive a share of the profit in form of dividends. Smart investors who have invested widely end in top performing companies end up earning handsome returns from dividends.

Thirdly, option trading has enabled investors to make good returns from stocks. Here, there is either option buying or option selling. In the case of option buying (calls or puts), investors grow their investment if stock prices move in one direction. Remember that in some cases, stock prices need to move significantly for investors to make money. On the other hand, option selling enables you to make money if the stock moves in three directions. With selling options, you can make money regardless of whether the stock goes downwards, increases in value or remains constant.

## Appendix I

### Worthless Stock: How to Avoid Doubling Your Losses

Con artists across the globe have stepped up their efforts to rip off investors, especially non-U.S. residents who have lost money in the U.S. securities markets. While it's natural to want to recoup one's losses as quickly and as fully as possible, the SEC warns investors to be extremely skeptical of offers to exchange worthless or poorly performing stocks for blue chips or "hot" performers.

Worthless stock is typically just that — worthless. And anyone who promises a quick way to recover from a bad investment is probably just lying to you. We encourage you to thoroughly investigate *any* investment opportunity, as well as the person promoting it, *before* you part with your money. This is especially critical if you are a non-U.S. investor seeking to invest in U.S. stocks — or if you learn about the opportunity over the telephone from a broker you don't know. The "broker" may well be a con artist, and the deal may be a dud. Remember, if an offer sounds too good to be true, it probably isn't true.

This alert tells you how to spot potential "stock swap" scams, how to evaluate the offers you hear about, and where to turn for help.

#### What to Watch Out For

Although fraudsters use a wide variety of techniques to carry out their "worthless stock swap" scams, most of these frauds boil down to a predictable formula: a persuasive pitch, which nearly always contains false assurances of legitimacy, followed by demands for money. Here are some "red flags" to avoid:

➤ **Aggressive Cold Calls from "Boiler-Rooms"** — Con artists posing as U.S. or United Kingdom brokers will first identify investors who have lost money investing in "microcap" stocks, the low-priced and thinly traded stocks issued by the smallest of U.S. companies. Operating from remote boiler-rooms, they then mount an aggressive cold calling or emailing campaign, focusing their pitch on loss recovery. They might offer to swap a poorly performing stock for an established, blue chip stock — or they will claim that their firm or an anonymous "client" wants to purchase the shares directly.

➤ **Impressive Websites Serving as Fronts for Virtual Offices** — To make their schemes appear convincing, fraudsters will invite you to visit "their" website — which will have pages of detailed information and perhaps a photo or biography of the broker. But all too often the site will be nothing more than a fraudulent copy of a legitimate firm's website — with changes made only to the name and contact information. The con artists will adopt fake yet familiar-sounding names and operate out of virtual offices, using phony addresses, remote mail drops, and redirected phone and facsimile numbers to carry out their scams.

➤ **Self-Provided References** — Knowing that regulators encourage investors to investigate before they invest, fraudsters often pretend to do the same. They will falsely assure you that the investment is properly registered with the appropriate agency and purport to give you the agency's telephone number so that you can verify that "fact." Sometimes they will give you the name of a real agency — other times they will fabricate one. But even if the agency does exist, the contact information invariably will be false. Instead of speaking with a government official, you'll reach the fraudsters or their colleagues — who will give the company, the promoter, or the transaction high marks.

➤ **Claims of Government "Approval"** — Another ruse fraudsters use to appear credible involves the misuse of federal agency seals, including the seals of the SEC and the Federal Trade Commission. They will copy the official seal from the regulator's website and use it to create fake letterhead for a fictitious letter of approval. But you should know that the SEC and FTC — like other state and federal regulators in the U.S. and around the world — do not "approve" or "endorse" any particular stock transactions or "loss recovery" programs.

➤ **Advance Payment Requests** — Regardless of how the fraudsters pitch their offers to "help", there's always a catch. Before they will complete the deal, they first will ask for an upfront "security deposit" or "margin payment" — or claim that you must post an "insurance" or "performance bond." The minute you pay the advance fee, the fraudsters nearly always disappear — leaving you with new losses. If you seem willing to make *further* payments, the con artists may instead keep asking for more — falsely claiming that the market price of the security has changed or that the payments will cover additional fees, taxes, bonds for the courier service, or other similar expenses. Only when you finally run out of patience or money to chase your losses do the fraudsters disappear for good.

## How to Protect Yourself

Regulators often refer to worthless stock scams as "recovery room operations," "advance fee schemes," or "reload scams" because the perpetrators prey on individuals who lost money once and are willing to invest even more in the hope of recovering their losses. Here are several ways to arm yourself against these thieving opportunists:

√ **Look Past Fancy Websites and Letterheads** – Anyone who knows how to "cut and paste" can create impressive, legitimate-looking websites and stationery at little to no cost. Don't be taken in by a glossy brochure, a glitzy website, or the presence of a regulator's official seal on a web page or document. The SEC does not authorize private companies to use our seal. If you see the SEC seal on a company's website or materials, think twice — and then think twice again.

√ **Be Skeptical of Government "Approval"** — Like most regulators around the world, the SEC does not evaluate the merits of any securities offering, nor do we determine whether a particular security is a "good" investment. Moreover, we never endorse specific firms, individuals, products, or services.

√ **Deal Only with Real Regulators** — Don't be fooled by those who tell you how and where to check out their credentials. Go straight to a *real* regulator for help. Here are the URLs you'll need to find your regulator:

**International Regulators** -- http://www.iosco.org/lists/

**U.S. Regulators --**

1. **SEC** -- http://www.sec.gov or http://www.sec.gov/contact.shtml
2. **FINRA** -- http://www.finra.org
3. **State Regulators** -- http://www.nasaa.org/ or http://www.nasaa.org/QuickLinks/ContactYourRegulator.cfm

**Caution:** If your contact provides any of these links electronically (in an email or on a website), do **not** simply click on those links. **Type the *full* URL into your web browser *yourself*.** Even though the URL looks right, a fraudster's link can take you to a very different destination.

√ **Independently Determine Whether the Offering Is Registered** -- In general, all securities offered in the U.S. must be registered with the SEC or qualify for an exemption. You can see whether a company has registered its securities with the SEC and download its disclosure documents using our EDGAR database.

√ **Check Out the Broker and the Firm** – Always verify whether the broker and the firm are properly licensed to do business in your state, province, or country. If the person claims to work at a U.S. brokerage firm, use FINRA's BrokerCheck website or call FINRA's Public Disclosure Program hotline at (800) 289-9999. If the person works elsewhere, contact the securities regulator for that country — and also for your home country, if more than one country is involved.

> **Tip:** Several international regulators list on their websites the names of unlicensed firms or entities that have allegedly targeted their citizens for worthless stock scams and other frauds.  Some sites that presently maintain these lists include:
>
> Australian Securities and Investment Commission
>
> Bermuda Monetary Authority
>
> Guernsey FSC
>
> Hong Kong Securities and Futures Commission
>
> Indonesian Capital Markets Supervisory Agency (BAPEPAM)
>
> Irish Financial Services Authority
>
> Isle of Man FSC
>
> Italian CONSOB
>
> Netherlands Authority for Financial Markets
>
> New Zealand Securities Commission
>
> Philippines SEC
>
> Spanish CNMV (click on "Investor Alerts" under "Cautions")
>
> Thailand Securities and Exchange Commission

> United Kingdom Financial Services
> Authority
>
> Please note that the SEC does not maintain or
> control these lists and cannot vouch for their
> accuracy.

✓ **Independently Verify References** – Never rely solely on references given to you by a broker you've never worked with before. The "international organizations" or "satisfied clients" they suggest you contact may well be part of the scam.

✓ **Be Wary of Unusual Banking Instructions** – Most reputable brokerage firms in the U.S. would not ask you to send your money to a non-U.S. bank — or to a U.S. bank for further credit to another bank or entity. In fact, a U.S. broker probably would not ever ask you to send payment to their bank at all.

**Where to Turn for Help**

If the case appears to involve a U.S. broker, please send your complaint in writing to the SEC using our Online Complaint Center. Be sure to include as many details as possible, including the names, addresses, telephone or fax numbers, and e-mail addresses or websites of any person or firm, the dates of each contact, and information on any specific representations and wire instructions provided by the broker.

Because many investment scams occur entirely outside the U.S., the SEC may not have jurisdiction to investigate and prosecute wrongdoers — even if the fraud involves stock issued by a U.S. company. If you run into trouble, contact the securities regulator for your home country and also the country where the broker does business.

**How to Get More Information**

If you want to invest wisely and steer clear of frauds, you must get the facts. Never, ever, make an investment based solely on a promoter's promises over the telephone or what you see on the Internet — especially if the investment involves a small, thinly-traded company that isn't well known. And don't even think about investing on your own in small companies that don't file regular reports with the SEC, unless you are willing to investigate each company thoroughly and to check the truth of every statement about the company.

For more information on investing wisely, please visit the Investor Information section of our website.

http://www.sec.gov/investor/pubs/worthless.htm, February 10, 2015

## Book Review

*Thank you for reading my book Basic Understanding of the Stock Market Book Four - for Teens and Young Adults. Please, if you liked the book take a spare moment as it would be a great help if you could post a review of it on Amazon and let other potential readers know why you liked it. It's not necessary to write a lengthy, formal review—a summary of the comments from you would be perfectly fine.*

## About the Author

Ronald E. Hudkins (1951-Present) now residing in Durango, Colorado was born in Canton, Ohio and raised in Massillon, Ohio. He was drafted into military service in 1970 where he remained up until 1993 when he retired honorably from the U.S. Army, Military Police Corps. During his service, after and in between a lot of traveling he attended many universities that include Kent State

University, Maryland University, Central Texas College (European Branch), Blair Junior College, Hagerstown Junior College and Phoenix University. He declared two majors in the areas of Business Administration and a Bachelor of Science in Information Technology.

The Author
Ronald E. Hudkins

Ronald has been writing as a hobby for over twenty years. He has completed a collection of multiple genres in both fiction and nonfiction that include financial, estate, cooking and identity theft. In the area of fiction he has published humor, science fiction and fantasy. He is polishing up some children's, paranormal romance, romance and additional science fiction books. He has approximately 50 additional plot outlines completed and their associated books in various stages of completion. We can anticipate more stories in the areas of finance, children's and young adult reading as well as humor, fantasy, romance, thrillers and even some mystery and steampunk. Only the author's files and mind know the definitive creations yet to be.

He is a Platinum Level Expert author at http://ezinearticles.com/expert=Ronald_Hudkins where he has published over 100 articles in 29 separate niches which have amassed over 74,000 views.

He participates on social sites, such as Facebook and Twitter, videos on YouTube and slid presentations too many and numerous to list. Needless to say, he stays occupied and busy and as such - we all benefit. See his other projects page on his author website at: http://www.ronaldhudkins.com

# Authors Other Books Fiction

| Book 3 | Book 4 |
|---|---|
| <br>Dec 21, 2013 | <br>Mar 20, 2013 |
| Book 5 | Book 7 |
| <br>Nov 16 2013 | 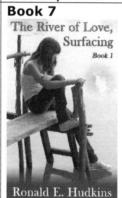<br>Pending Apr 2015 |
| Book16 | Book 17 |
| <br>Aug 28, 2014 | 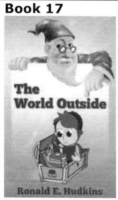<br>Sep 16, 2014 |
| | |

**Book 9**

Mar 19, 2014

## Authors Other Books Nonfiction

**Book 6**

Dec 26, 2013

**Book 13**

Ronald E. Hudkins

Aug 12, 2014

**Book 12**

Ronald E. Hudkins

Aug 22, 2014

**Book 8**

Mar 7, 2014

**Book 19**

Feb 10, 2015

**Book 20**

Pending Feb 2015

**Book 11**

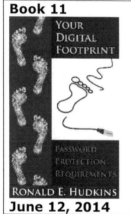

June 12, 2014

**Book 18**

Jan 20, 2015

**Book 14**

Oct 27, 2014

**Book 1**

Jul 12, 2007

| Book 2 | Just for Fun |
|---|---|
|  | |
| Jun 15, 2011 | Humor Magazine |

## Authors Adult Books Romance/Erotica

| Book 10 | Book 15 |
|---|---|
| 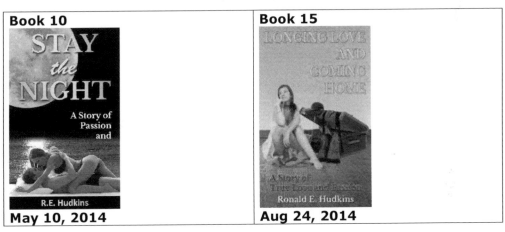 | |
| May 10, 2014 | Aug 24, 2014 |

See author's wholesale and retail outlets at the following site;

RONALDHUDKINS.COM

**The Author's Books are generally available in the following formats;**

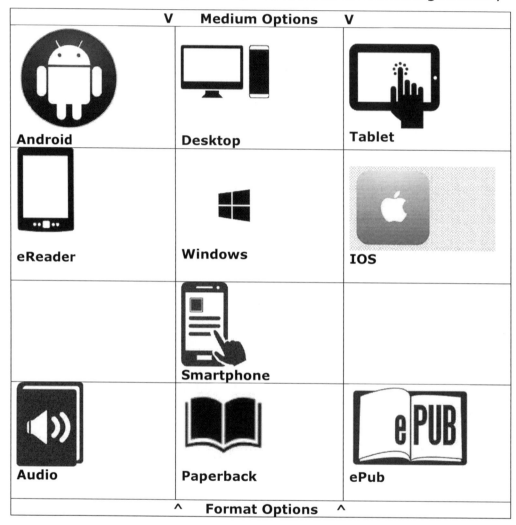

| V Medium Options V | | |
|---|---|---|
| Android | Desktop | Tablet |
| eReader | Windows | IOS |
| | Smartphone | |
| Audio | Paperback | ePub |
| ^ Format Options ^ | | |

**Thank You for the Visit !!!**

**Investing for Profit**

If you are looking for some of the very best investment programs and services relative to Commodities, Forex, Options, Personal Finance, Real Estate and Stocks this page has you covered. Remember, the right knowledge can mean the difference between significant gains and catastrophic losses. We're here to give you the right knowledge for each market.

## About Investing for Profit

If you are guessing or simply do not know what you are doing in the world of investment you can lose a lot of your hard earned money. Sure, you can get lucky and actually establish some profitable investments but you can also see your profits get wiped out in an instant. However with the proper guidance, tools and self-help education you can learn to limit any losses in any market and these reference books are designed specifically to show you how.

When you visit my Investing for Profit digital library you will find the absolute top of the line investment programs and services that are currently or about to be available. It does not matter where your interests are held be it in Stocks, FOREX, options, real estate or stocks this site will keep you investing intelligently. You know as well as I the difference between exceptional gains or disastrous losses boils down to just having the correct knowledge. At this site you have the complete and correct knowledge no matter which market you invest in.

One of the best things about the Investing for Profit Mall is the selection of programs that are available. Different sectors and trading styles can be hot at various times. When there is a bull market in natural gas, gold or oil you can check out the many featured programs in the commodities trading area. If the stock market is sinking maybe other investment option programs are right for you. This site allows you to educate yourself completely for whatever market you choose to place your investments.

So go ahead, look around and find the investing strategies that are right for you. (http://digijunction.com/investing/guard1)

Also, please be sure to bookmark this site as we make updates with the newest and hottest programs often.

---

References

Appendix I, U.S. Treasury Department
http://www.sec.gov/investor/pubs/worthless.htm, February 10, 2015

61954745R00119

Made in the USA
Middletown, DE
17 January 2018